SMALL BOATS

SMALL BOATS
by Philip C. Bolger

International Marine Publishing Company
Camden, Maine

Dedicated

to

Lindsay Lord, Naval Architect
Falmouth Foreside, Maine

CONTENTS

PREFACE

Some of these designs were commissioned, for love or money, but most of them started with soft-penciled doodles done when I should have been plugging away on the plans of something bigger and more elaborate. I offer them in the same spirit, hoping that for each person who builds one of these boats, a hundred will get some amusement of an evening imagining themselves building or sailing one. I've seen some tragedies come of over-ambitious amateur boatbuilding, and even a little boat can be a loathsome thing if it hangs around interminably and looks more and more as though it would be a messy, unsalable job if it ever was finished. Most of these designs are meant for people who like carpentry at least as much as boating; the other sort, with whom I'm in sympathy, are well-advised to buy their boats, or get out in somebody else's boat.

Books like this one tend to hang around indefinitely, no matter whether they're good or bad. If you're reading this in the year 2025, you might bear in mind that not only have I been dead for quite some time, but also if I found a mistake in any of these plans in, say 1975, I have no way to let you know about it. Be sure there are some; it's up to a builder to catch and correct them.

Probably the 2025 reader won't be intending to use any of the designs, except for the light dory, in any case, because he won't feel up to tackling the foot-inch English measurement system used. I'd like to assure him that this isn't a perversity of mine; believe it or not, it's a fact that it was hard to find a builder in English America who would work with metric plans when this book was written. Almost all were so accustomed to dividing the length of the first joint of King Edward the First's thumb into eight and sixteen parts for all their measurements that they were completely unconscious of the amount of time they were wasting. King Edward's thumb-joint was 2.54 centimeters long; the dimension given as ¾″ (three-quarters of an inch) is almost exactly nineteen millimeters (not that any dimension in the book needs to be accurate to anything like a millimeter) , and a cheap slide rule will reduce most of the material sizes to rational scale fairly easily. If anybody brought up on metrics badly wants to use one of these English-scale plans, I'd say it will work better to buy an English scale and puzzle out how to use it long enough to get the lofting done full size, rather than try to translate a table of offsets. For casual comparisons, convert the dimension given into inches and multiply by 2.54; thus 19'10" (nineteen feet, ten inches) equals 228 plus 10 inches, 238, times 2.54 equals 6.05 meters. Never mind the fractions of inches; that way lies madness.

I think the names of the designs are easier to keep track of than the numbers. Kotick was the white seal in the Kipling story of that name; a Mippet is a bird invented by Angela Thirkell for the bird-watchers of Barsetshire; the Prancing Pony was the inn at Bree in *The Lord of the Rings*. Most of the others will yield to a big dictionary or geographical gazetteer. Many of them were named by owners and builders, but I had better take the responsibility for Archaeopteryx, "an extinct primitive bird with reptilian characteristics."

Philip C. Bolger

SMALL BOATS

1

AMESBURY SKIFF MIPPET

$$9'6'' \times 3'6''$$

When I was eleven or twelve years old, I paid twenty dollars for a boat much like this one. At the time, Amesbury skiffs as small as this were thought to be impractical; she had probably been built for a child originally. She was a very graceful and generally nice little boat, but the type was commonplace and it didn't occur to me to make a drawing of her or even keep a photo. The design here is from memory plus such alterations as seemed good to me, such as more rocker in the bottom profile. Amesbury skiffs, dories too for that matter, tended to be too straight along the bottom to be ideal for easy rowing, because it was hard to make their thick bottom planking hold the curve, especially where the outboard planks feathered out toward the ends of the boat.

Boats with narrow bottoms and long overhangs, like this, don't carry well for their length, or aren't compact for their capacity, whichever way you want it, but they do tend to be dry in a chop and somewhat forgiving of an over-load. One time there were five boys in my old skiff. She had about two inches of freeboard left amidships. One held the oars, two sat in the stern and gripped the oars outboard of the handles, one sat ahead with his hands on the oarsman's shoulders, and the last perched on the stem with hands on *his* shoulders. We all pushed and pulled together. Our swaying back and forth dipped the bow and the stern alternately to the water's edge, but her high sheer kept her afloat for quite some time, 'till we met a dragger plowing home with forty thousand pounds of haddock. In her wake our oars floated gently up out of the rowlocks and we swam the boat ashore.

This new design, with lighter construction and more rockered bottom, might just barely have got away with that; at any rate she is certainly a much safer and drier proposition than the usual tiny blunt-bowed dinghy for, say, three adults maximum. With a single man, or a woman and two small children, or some such load, she will live in a really terrifying sea if the oarsman has some idea of what he (or she) is about.

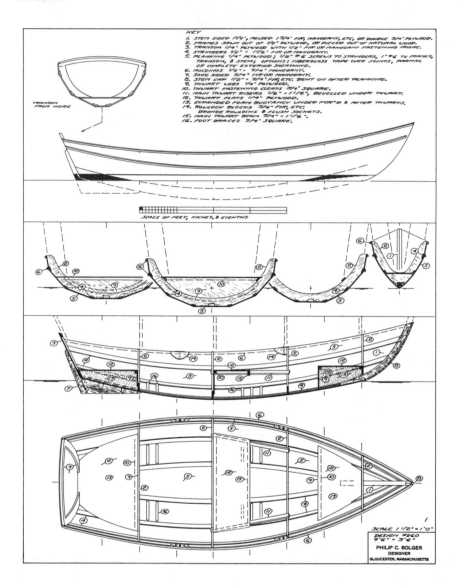

Also, with a reasonable load, she is a pleasant boat to row as long as you don't try to row her fast. She's too short for that, or to carry her way well by real rowboat standards, but using a short, quick stroke she can be kept moving very nicely at three miles an hour or so. I once covered over a hundred miles in four days in a boat nowhere near as good, in smooth water and with some help from a fair stream, it's true. Six-foot oars are long enough for a boat as low-sided at the locks as this one.

Though an awkward thing to take on board a smallish cruiser, she will tow light and dry at nearly any speed and in nearly any kind of sea, not much hindrance to even a very small cruiser and, I should say, by no means detrimental to "the style of the equipage."

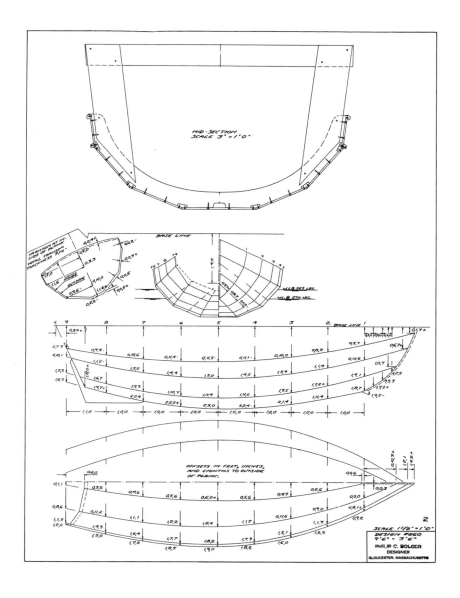

2
POOHSTICKS

11'4" x 3'10"

My brother and I were sitting in the cockpit of my sloop *Blacksnake*, watching my small nephew try to row a punt I had at the time. The punt was a miserable thing to start with, and was foul at that, which made his progress painful to watch. We talked of how a generation was growing up with no idea that there was such a thing as a good rowboat, and he offered to build a rowing boat for his children if I would get out a design along lines he had in mind. The boat that resulted is still in fine shape, though the small boy she was built for is practicing law. The plans have been redrawn twice, once to correct a few things that weren't quite right in the first ones, and again after the second set met with an accident in an editorial office, but I've never been tempted to alter the shape of the hull. The curve of the keel looks excessive when she is under construction, bottom up, but it isn't; I'd give her more if I wasn't afraid it would make her tender. The sides have more twist than I usually allow now in a plywood boat, but apparently there hasn't been any trouble caused; at least none of the many people who've built them have complained about it.

The boat is meant for children; that is, for a very light load. Once the total displacement goes much over 250 pounds, the resistance starts to build up because of eddies around and under the chine as it gets into the water. Still, she goes much better than one might think with an overload, on account of the sharp stern. I know of a large man with a very large wife who use one of these; the pair of them certainly go over 400 pounds, yet she runs along very well. Lightly loaded, in smooth water, a strong man or boy who knows how to row can get a tremendous spurt of speed out of a model like this.

I've drawn seven-foot oars on the plans to make sure they can be stowed, but 6'6" is actually about the right length for average circumstances. I heard about a trial with a pair of ten-foot oars, first as a pair, cross-handed, then staggered forward on one side and aft on the other, two hands to an

Three versions of Poohsticks

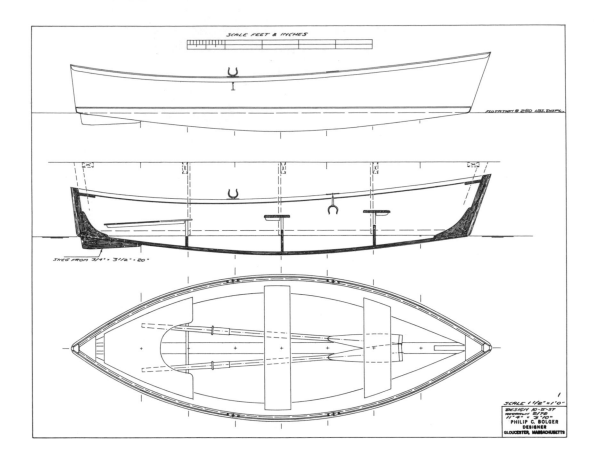

oar; probably she went quite fast, especially the second way if they had something to steer with, but I didn't hear that the normal oars were abandoned afterwards.

Some years ago I was anchored in a pretty cove when two auxiliaries came in for the night and turned their owners' young daughters loose in two noisy little outboard dinghies. That's how four beautiful girl-children came to remind me, that one time, of a swarm of houseflies. I'm persuaded that they would have had more fun for themselves, and improved their health, besides adding to the beauty of the surroundings, if they'd had a couple of these rowing boats instead of the noise-makers. They tow easily and are good at staying on top of the water when light, and although they are inconveniently long to take on board most boats, one can generally figure a way to angle the pointed stern into some corner or other.

This was the first design I made using the outside chine log, which I've since adopted quite often in constant-deadrise boats; it saves some labor in fitting the log, and gives a better bearing and fastening for the size of the log. It also gains a bit of stability, and I have an idea, just conjecture, that

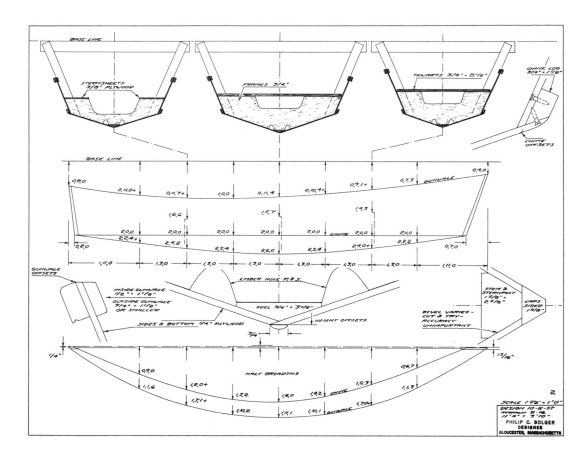

it reduces eddying along under the chine by carrying the side flow aft. Otherwise, I take it the construction is clear enough. It would be easy to save some weight in the frames and thwarts, but the solid ones shown are simple, and pleasant to the eye.

For a hard-chine plywood boat, and such a tiny one, this craft has some elegance, of a yachty type at that. People who have built them have tended to go in for fancy finish and niceties of various kinds. One had graceful laminated knees in place of the square-across breasthooks shown. Some carved work has been done around the thwarts, or a "laid deck" substituted for the plywood stern-sheets, or oversize flag staffs mounted bow and stern. The original one had her stem extended a few inches above the sheer and carved as the head of Winnie-the-Pooh. We *are* supposed to be having fun, are we not?

3

DEFENDER

11'0" x 3'10"

This boat was meant to resemble an 1890-vintage yacht tender, the sort of thing you used to see hanging in side davits on medium-size schooner yachts. Originally she was going to have an all-bright finish, but wiping up slopped glue became so frustrating that Ben Dolloff, who built her, decided he preferred white paint, which I liked better in the first place.

As dinghies go nowadays she's a big and powerful boat. She can carry six people in smooth water if they hold still, and would live in a middling seaway with four. As the photo suggests, one man alone can get around quite fast in her, and with two or three people she can be rowed six miles in two hours in calm weather. However she was not intended for rowing long distances, so I gave her a high and flaring bow to enable her to go against a head sea without shipping water; in fact she's a very fair surfboat for her length. The combination of strongly rockered keel, full lines in the upper part of the bow, and a hard bilge amidships gives her good reserve buoyancy characteristics; it's possible to get out of her over the bow with much less risk of a swim than in most dinghies.

The skeg is drawn very large to keep her straight at high towing speeds, and the sides are full enough to avoid scooping her full of water if she slews into the quarter wave. She cocks her bow up high if towed fast, but the towing drag doesn't seem to be great, even for a small auxiliary.

She's not a good model for even a very small outboard motor and it seems to me that it would be foolishness to go to this much trouble for a yacht-like appearance and then spoil the effect with a motor. As for sailing her, of course it could be done; for instance the leeboards, rudder, and rig of the *Fieldmouse* design could be adapted to this hull with the mast stepped about Station #3 and the leeboards pivoted between #6 and #7. A sprit rig like that of the Thomaston Galley would perhaps be more sensible on account of the much shorter mast, but the trouble with any sailing rig, apart from the considerable expense, is that the gear for it makes a great clutter

Defender *light*

Defender *loaded*

in the boat that spoils her for rowing. Even the short mast of the sprit rig won't stow out of the way in a boat as short as this. She is a good all-around model for sailing, however, only a trifle weak in the quarters as compared with a good frostbite type, say an Alden X, which I always thought was the best of them.

The glued lapstrake plywood construction designed is basically very light, and I think it would be possible to build one of these to weigh not much over 90 pounds. This might involve leaving out half or more of the bent frames, which I regard as mostly decorative in any case, and it certainly would involve leaving out a lot of rather thick solid mahogany knees and thwarts that found their way into the one shown, along with the pretty

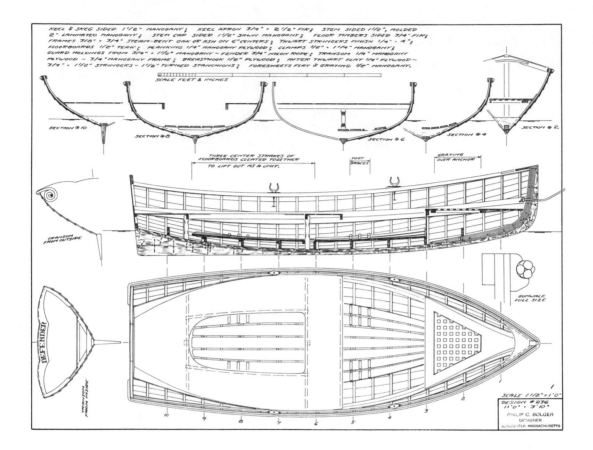

grating and teak floorboards. As built, I judged she weighed 140 pounds
or more after helping to carry her around, which is more than I'd call ideal
for a boat of her type, though it's still less than her fiberglass equivalent. I
must say that most of the things that add weight to her also add beauty and
a fine feeling of solidity.

Many of the period yacht tenders of this type were built carvel because it
was silent among the ripples at night; such boats were prone to leak hor-
ribly, but with modern seam compounds it ought to be possible to do better.
A very good boat this shape could be built strip-planked, but it's almost
impossible to build a boat that way that inspires admiration at really close
range, so it wouldn't suit the original purpose of the design.

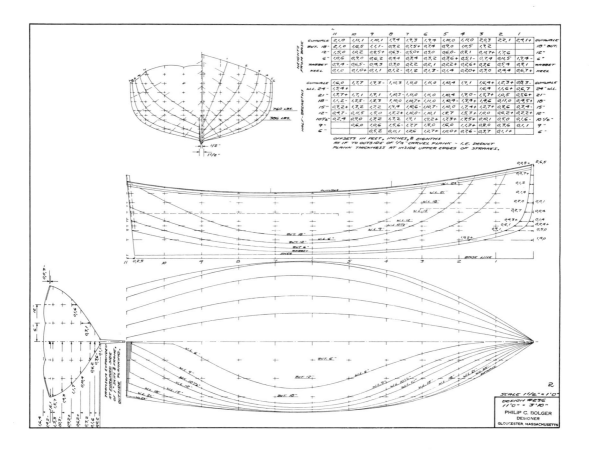

OFFSETS IN FEET, INCHES, & EIGHTHS
AS IF TO OUTSIDE OF 1/4" CARVEL PLANK — I.E. DEDUCT
PLANK THICKNESS AT INSIDE UPPER EDGES OF STRAKES.

SCALE 1 1/2" = 1'0"
DESIGN #236
11'0" = 3'10"
PHILIP C. BOLGER
DESIGNER
GLOUCESTER, MASSACHUSETTS

4

LIGHT DORY TYPE V

4.74 meters by 1.22 meters

The first slimmed-down dory I designed was back in the early fifties, a planked boat with slightly rounded sides. The few that were built went very well but there wasn't much interest and I did no more about it for eight or ten years, when I needed a towing tender for my cruising sharpie *Pointer* and built myself a plywood version of the earlier boat. This attracted so much attention around anchorages that I redesigned it for production and speculated moderately profitably on a run of a hundred of them, built by Art Rand's shop in Ipswich with his characteristic beautiful finish. They were very much admired for their grace and speed, and, though they were terribly tender and tippy, they would go through all kinds of dirty weather perfectly dry and bring you home safe and happy as long as you had sense enough not to stand up to admire the view. Notable yachtsmen and captains of industry bought them, several designers brought out more or less altered versions, and a West Coast builder of elastic ethics introduced a fiberglass copy using one of mine for a mold plug.

Later on I redesigned it still again for Capt. Jim Orrell, the Texas Dory man; it was he who called it the Gloucester Gull and the plans continue to be available at very modest prices from him and from Harold H. Payson, South Thomaston, Maine 04858, who also builds them on a cash and carry basis. This is certainly the best design I ever made: when I come up for judgment and they stop me at the gate and ask "what's your excuse?" I'll tell them I designed the Gloucester Light Dory and they'll have to let me in.

I no longer own those plans, so I thought I would design another one for this book and take the chance to put the plans into metric scale and units; besides, I've thought up some changes that may or may not be a case of not knowing when to let well enough alone. If you prefer the earlier version, or feel resistant to my arguments about the superiority of the metric system, you can write Harold Payson.

The new design has slightly more rocker in its bottom and hence is deeper, with less flare. The midsection is moved aft, making the lines of the bow sharper and the stern blunter. The pointed stern seemed to me to be easier to build than the triangular tombstone, after the impatient, sloppy carpenter that I am had problems getting all the bevels right in the latter. There is less twist in the sides. The external chine log seems slightly easier to fit than the conventional type, leaves a clean interior, and adds a minute amount to the stability, which certainly needs anything it can get; I don't think it increases the resistance but I can't prove it yet.

The thwarts have been placed closer together to lighten up the ends. With the sharper bow, I have hopes that her ability to go against a head sea may be noticeably better, light or loaded. Also, the forward rowing position, which was too low and without enough spread at the locks, will certainly be better. To get these improvements I gave away the luxurious lounging position that was possible for a passenger in the stern in the older design.

About the only other change of any significance, apart from the optional (and well-tested) lighter construction indicated, is the introduction of positive buoyancy. I never came near swamping one of these myself, or saw one come near it, and I've been in them or with them in some wicked water ranging from the rapids of the Kootenai River to the north shore of Buzzards Bay in a southerly gale. (It's true that I lost my balance and fell in the sea under embarrassing circumstances one time, but the boat just snapped back and laughed at me, not shipping a drop.) Nevertheless, Murphy's Law ("If something *can* go wrong, it *will*.") is as sound as ever and the buoyancy might be a comfort. Besides, interfering bureaucrats are beginning to get around to rowboats in their statutory duties of trying to make the world foolproof, and we may as well anticipate them where possible. I wouldn't advise anybody to step on these small end decks! It is possible to step out of one of these boats over the bow, as at a crowded float. The boat feels terribly tender when the stern cocks up high, but actually has more reserve stability in that attitude than in normal trim; if you hold on so she can't dump you in the water, and make a long stride from the end of the bottom to the float, she won't go over, or ship any water.

I've seen several attempts to arrange sailing rigs and motors on boats of this type, all of which seemed to me to result in extremely uncomfortable, inefficient, and outright dangerous boats. The Sea Hawk Dory Skiff shows what I think an outboard of this type should be like, and *Featherwind* is a sailing version; the Thomaston Galley shows how far out I think you must go to combine any two functions efficiently, and even in that I could not save the rough-water capability. Jim Orrell, who was irritated when I refused to design a sailing rig for the Gloucester Gull, got somebody in Scotland to devise a very small boom lugsail for it, using an oar for a leeboard; if you must make a fool of yourself trying to sail one of these, that's the way to go, but I'll have no part of it.

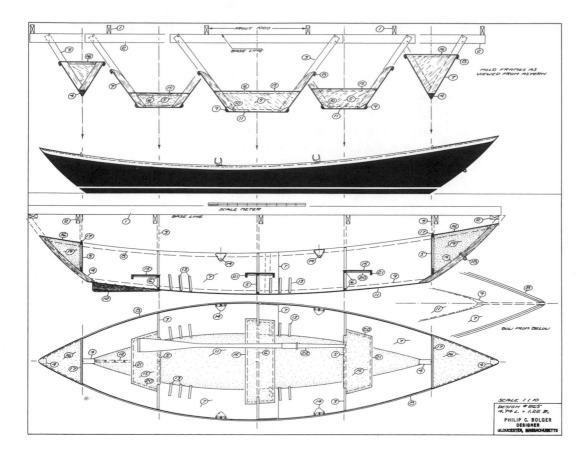

This design may or may not be an improvement on the predecessor many people have been pleased to call a classic, but I think it is good enough to be worth building for a long time to come, maybe even when the metric system is common in North America.

KEY TO PLANS

1.   Base timbers 40 mm x 90 mm or heavier; may be dispensed with if a flat wood floor or other good base is available.

2.   Mold crosspieces 40 mm x 90 mm, more or less as convenient.

3.   Side frames about 20 mm x 60 mm, extended to base crosspieces; after hull is righted, sawn off and faired out to gunwale about as shown; screw or bolt to crosspieces.

4.   Stem and sternpost glued up from eight layers of 6 mm plywood, or the equivalent, to finish sided about 48 mm; molded 50 mm; bevel will vary slightly.

5.   End bulkheads and bottom webs 6 mm plywood.

6.   Fastening cleats of webs and bulkheads 20 mm x 20 mm.

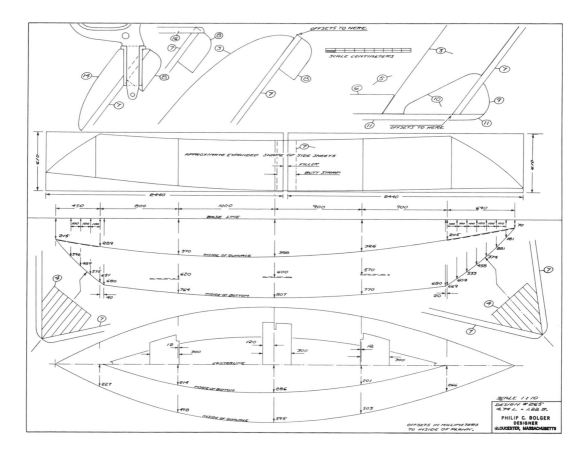

7. Side planking 6 mm plywood; the expansion given is not very exact, but shows sheet usage; butt strap is 20 cm wide; put sides on molds roughly shaped and cut down to chine and gunwale marks on molds and end posts.

8. Gunwale stringers 20 mm x 40 mm, sprung over sides to marked points and clamped, with glue and screws or nails, to sides which can then be trimmed down flush with the edges.

9. Chine logs same as gunwale stringers except for greater bevelling required —see full-scale section.

10. Drainage openings; also make sure the small limbers in the end bulkheads are not lost in bevelling and can be kept clear.

11. Bottom 6 mm plywood; if preferred, may be thicker up to 12 mm or may be sheathed with one, two, or more layers of plastic; get out from a 122 cm x 366 cm sheet without butts.

12. Skeg about 20 mm x 90 mm x 710 mm, well rounded off and faired; four 50 mm and three 20 mm round-head screws from inside.

13. Foot braces 20 mm x 20 mm, glued to sides.

14. Rowlock socket blocks from 20 mm x 110 mm x 110 mm, glued and screwed very strongly in place; sockets standard 12.5 mm to fit standard rowlocks as well as special type shown.

15.   Thwarts 6 mm plywood.

16.   End decks 6 mm plywood; see full-size section for bevel of gunwales under decks.

17.   Coamings 20 mm x 20 mm bevelled inside.

18.   Stem eyebolt about 10 mm x 60 mm bronze, for painter attachment.

19.   Overhangs filled with expanded or cut urethane foam; positive buoyancy here will ensure floating upright when swamped; optionally, some additional foam can be placed under the for'd and after thwarts and under the midship thwart abaft its web, adding about 45 kilos to the positive buoyancy of the boat and making it substantially easier to bail out when swamped.

20.   Cleats on sides about 20 mm x 20 mm to support ends of thwarts.

21.   Thwart edge stiffeners about 20 mm x 40 mm.

Plywood is all 6 millimeter, fir or mahogany, marine grade if readily available, with veneer voids carefully plugged in any case.

Natural wood may be mahogany, Douglas fir, or any moderately hard wood having good gluing characteristics; avoid oak, teak, and yellow pine. Dimensions, in millimeters if not specified, are nowhere critical and may be varied as convenient and according to judgment of expected wear and tear. The 6 mm plywood would be a minimum for ordinary use; maximum in boats considered successful has been 10 mm sides and 12.5 mm bottom, without sheathing; a hull with those thicknesses weighs about 56 kilos.

The strength of the boat should be in the gluing, and if it is well done any convenient screws or nails may be used, but bronze or Everdur screws of good thickness are best; most would be 20 mm, with a few longer where fastening depth permits.

5

VICTORIA

15'6" x 4'2"

Boating magazine ran a feature article about a rowing boat I had built
while working in Spain, and got a flood of letters, around 1,500, I understand, wanting to buy the plans. I did not think the design was suitable for
general use and refused to release it, so the editors commissioned this design
as a substitute. It was supposed to be as versatile as possible: light enough
for one person alone to haul up onto a trailer easily or drag up a beach;
buoyant enough to carry a family and stable enough to stand up in or
clamber out of over the stemhead; not too short to be rowed fast when
necessary, or so fragile that she shouldn't be beached or taken into floating
ice; able enough to cope with a fair chop but not so high-ended as to be
blown out of control in strong winds; incidentally, as elegant as possible
to the eye.

She's particularly suitable for the type of rowing in which two or three
people row one at a time. In calm weather it's possible to cover as much as
thirty miles a day in this manner without any athletic pretensions or ex-
haustion. I should say, though, that some practice is needed; I tend to forget
that rowing does call for some skill and to be surprised when some strong-
looking boy takes his strokes with the oar blades at the wrong angle, so that
they hop up out of the locks, or corrects his course with the wrong oar and
ends up eight points off course, or pulls round-shouldered and develops a
backache after an hour or two. All this tends to discourage a beginner who
hasn't been warned that there's anything to learn, and, when you add on all
the people whose only experience has been in boats and with gear of impossible proportions, it's no wonder that so few people take rowing seriously
as transportation or recreation.

I'm persuaded that for casual rowing with a single oarsman *Victoria* is
close to the optimum length; it's the racing over short courses that has produced the very long rowing boats and even they have tended to be shortened
up in recent years. Even when fairly heavily loaded, *Victoria* makes no

The Spanish-built pulling boat

appreciable waves except when she is rowed by two men both working at a pace they can't keep up long; it follows that more length would just add wetted surface in normal use, especially as two-pair rowing is an efficient use of energy only when bucking a strong head wind. On the other hand a much shorter boat, like the *Defender* design, is apt to suffer from eddy-making when it's loaded deep.

The construction indicated has been common for many years in England; it's particularly good from a maintenance point of view, besides being light for its strength. Others are mentioned below. By the way, for those who have little or no experience with lofting, H. I. Chapelle's book, *Boatbuilding* (New York: Norton), has the most complete and lucid manual of lofting practice available.

KEY TO CONSTRUCTION

Plywood to be exterior grade, or marine grade if available, smooth both sides, Douglas fir, mahogany, or mahogany-faced.

Natural wood, understood if not specified as plywood, may be any convenient timber having good gluing and reasonably good screw-holding properties. Oak, teak, or yellow pine are undesirable; Douglas fir, Philippine or other mahogany, white cedar or white pine, or good-quality spruce, are all suitable.

The designed structure depends on the use of high-grade, slow-setting, waterproof marine glue not requiring high pressure or heat for setting.

1. Keel plank from $\frac{3}{4}''$ x $3\frac{1}{2}''$, sprung to fore-and-aft shape; note that it runs straight for the last couple of feet at the forward end, the rocker there being bevelled off the underside.

2. Stem laminated from $\frac{1}{4}''$ x $1\frac{1}{4}''$ to finish $1\frac{1}{4}''$ x $1\frac{1}{2}''$; thinner courses may be used if available timber is too stiff to take the bend cold, or thicker courses

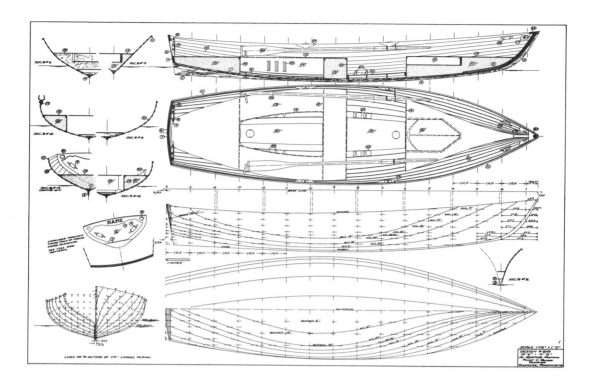

may be steamed or boiled if allowed to dry out before gluing.

3. Stem cap may be laminated same as stem, or applied in short sawn sections; in either case it is to be installed after planking, and the part forward of the fore end of the keel may be screwed on without glue to be easily removed if damaged.

4. Keel shoe (see full-size sections) from 15/16″ x 1¼″ through the middle part of the hull, sprung in after planking.

5. Skeg from 1¼″ by about 5½″ by about 5′ long, tapered about as shown. May be shod full-length with ½″ bronze half-oval.

6. Transom ¼″ plywood.

7. Transom frame laminated from three courses of ¼″ by about 4″ maximum; intended to be built on a jig consisting of a ½″ plywood pattern cut to the lofted or given inside shape and bent on heavy radius forms to the given curve; the four layers of frame and transom, glued up together on the jig, will hold their shape when removed and set up to take the planking.

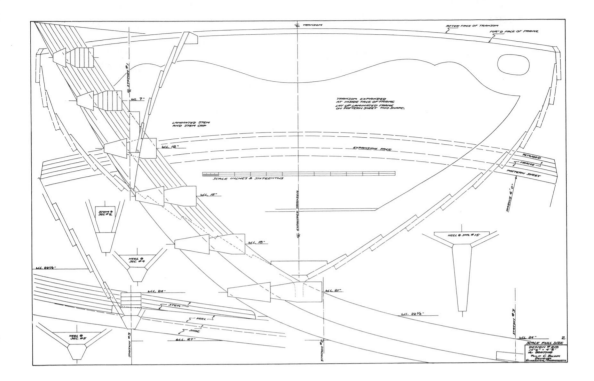

8.   Hawseholes cut through frame and transom, well rounded off inside and out.

9.   Six-inch wood cleats glued on and with four 1″ screws each from outside.

10.   Planking ¼″ plywood lapstrake, with 1″ overlap carried the full length as shown; eleven strakes to a side, with widths scaled roughly from the section drawings and the lay corrected and faired on the molds. The offsets are given to outside of plank on account of other optional constructions; i.e. in designed construction deduct plank thickness from molds at points where the strakes bear, at inside upper edges of strakes. (In perfectionist lofting, plank deductions will be taken from diagonals, but the difference amounts to only about 1/32″ in the upper part of the bow, which is the maximum.) The full lap is to be carried past the transom as shown; on the stem, shiplap (requires a rabbet plane) or bevelled dory-lap may be used. The planking is secured with about ¾″ screws at stem, keel, and transom; if the gluing is well done, the laps need no metal fastenings, but may be riveted or clinch-nailed if there is doubt about the glue. Natural wood *must not* be used in this frameless structure as it will eventually split along the laps.

11.   Gunwale molding ½″ x ¾″ for most of the length; in way of the flared bow, it is still ¾″ vertically but must be worked from a thicker section as shown to retain ½″ projection; there is no special advantage in having this molding in one section the full length.

12.   Bulkheads ¼″ plywood, fitted after hull is planked and turned over;

glued in place without other fastenings to planking; leave drainage space at each lap to prevent trapping water.

13. Seat flats ¼″ plywood, screwed down on ½″ x ¾″ cleats glued and screwed to planking in short lengths as convenient; these flats will need stiffening beams if not supported by foam as indicated.

14. Faces of fore and aft seats ¼″; make sure that these don't meet the planking so neatly that they trap water.

15. Expanded, sprayed, or cut-block foam, preferably urethane, under seat flats; provides support for the flats and enough positive buoyancy to allow the boat to be bailed out while still afloat if swamped.

16. Recess in foam, with removable top, to stow anchor (ten pound yachtsman-type suggested) and roding.

17. Hawsehole cut through planking and reinforcing blocks inside, all well rounded off.

18. Cleats as on transom.

19. Rowlocks bronze flush-socket type, set in 1¼″ blocks well glued and further secured with 1¼″ screws driven from outside.

20. Oars to suit; eight-foot Old Town spruce spoons shown, which are efficient but slightly brittle. It is suggested that the second pair be ash straight-blades, which are stronger and cheaper though not so pleasant to use; one or both pairs to be fitted with racks and lanyards to stow out of the way, more or less as shown.

21. Floorboards ¼″ plywood with stiffening cleats about as shown placed to take weight mostly on the top of the keel plank; boards laid loose with small cleats as needed to keep them from sliding; the round holes shown are handholes for lifting out.

22. Foot braces from 1¼″ x 1½″, glued to seat fronts; place by experiment.

23. Forward foot braces glued to inside of planking; similar to after ones but with ¼″ pads added to protect planking.

24. Breasthook ¾″ x 3½″ x 5⅝″; secure with glue to stem and planking and with at least six 1¾″ or longer screws driven from outside, to be strong enough to lift the boat.

Alternate constructions

A. Carvel planking ¼″ to ⅜″, using thiokol seam compound; frames steam-bent ash or oak, ½″ x ¾″ on about six, to eight-inch centers. B. Framed lap-strake using either plywood or natural wood, as shown but with ½″ x ¾″ bent frames on about 12″ centers. C. Cold-molded plywood using three veneer courses to finish 3/16″, with or without plastic sheathing; no frames; bulkheads, etc., about as designed. D. Glued and edge-nailed strip construction with strips ¼″ x ½″, or 5/16″ x ⅝″, or ⅜″ x ¾″ (width of strips is controlled by having to drive a nail through two and into a third across the curving surface; in other words the thinner the planking, the narrower the strips must be and the more labor to set them); bulkheads, etc., about as designed. All the wood constructions have the designed stem, keel, and transom structure. All except "C" will be heavier for the same strength than the designed construction; cold-molding would be the best construction functionally of all, but is apt to be expensive and ugly.

With some slight modifications along the keel and skeg this model is very well suited to fiberglass-reinforced plastic construction, but in my opinion, as of 1970, this construction is justifiable only when fairly large production is intended.

It would take a very skilled metalworker to produce an aluminum boat this shape that was fair, even though riveted rather than welded.

HEIGHTS FROM BASE LINE

	16	15	14	13	12	11	10	9	8	7	6	5	4	3	2	1
GUNWALE	0.8.2	0.9.4	0.10.3	0.11.0	0.11.4-	0.11.5	0.11.5-	0.11.3+	0.11.0	0.10.4-	0.9.6	0.9.0-	0.8.0	0.7.0	0.5.7	0.4.5
BUTTOCK 18"			1.4.1+	1.7.2	1.9.5	1.11.2	2.0.0+	2.0.0	1.11.0+	1.9.1+	1.6.0	1.1.4+	0.9.0			
12"	1.3.1	1.6.1+	1.8.7	1.11.2-	2.1.0	2.2.2	2.2.7-	2.2.6+	2.2.2-	2.0.7	1.10.7+	1.7.6+	1.3.2+	0.10.0		
6"	1.7.1	1.9.6	2.0.0+	2.2.0-	2.3.2+	2.4.2	2.4.6-	2.4.5	2.4.3-	2.3.4+	2.2.2	2.0.3	1.9.4	1.4.7	0.10.3	
RABBET	1.10.0	2.0.4-	2.2.4	2.4.0+	2.5.1-	2.5.6-	2.6.0	2.6.1	2.6.0+	2.5.6-	2.5.1-	2.4.2-	2.3.0	2.1.4	1.10.5+	1.0.2
SKEG ETC.	2.3.6+	2.4.3	2.4.7+	2.5.4	2.6.0	2.6.4-	2.6.6	2.6.7	2.6.6+	2.6.4-	2.5.7-	2.5.0-	2.3.6	2.2.2	1.11.7+	1.2.4

HALF BREADTHS

	16	15	14	13	12	11	10	9	8	7	6	5	4	3	2	1
GUNWALE	1.3.4+	1.6.0-	1.8.0	1.9.6	1.11.0+	2.0.0	2.0.5	2.0.7+	2.0.6+	2.0.3	1.11.3+	1.9.5+	1.7.0	1.3.2-	0.10.1	0.3.6
W.L. 9"	1.3.4-											1.9.5	1.6.0+	1.1.0	0.7.0+	0.1.3+
12"	1.2.7	1.5.4+	1.7.7	1.9.6	1.11.0+	2.0.0	2.0.5	2.0.7+	2.0.6	2.0.0-	1.10.2	1.7.2+	1.3.1	0.10.0+	0.4.6+	0.0.5+
15"	1.0.1	1.3.6+	1.6.7	1.9.1	1.10.6	1.11.7	2.0.4	2.0.5	2.0.2-	1.10.6	1.8.3	1.4.6+	1.0.2	0.7.4-	0.3.2-	
18"	0.8.0-	1.0.2	1.4.1	1.7.2+	1.9.4+	1.11.0	1.11.5+	1.11.6	1.10.7	1.9.0	1.6.0	1.2.0-	0.9.3-	0.5.2	0.2.0	
21"	0.2.4	0.7.4-	0.11.7-	1.3.6	1.6.7-	1.8.6+	1.9.6+	1.9.6	1.8.4+	1.6.2	1.2.6-	0.10.4+	0.6.4-	0.3.2+	0.1.1	
22½"	0.0.5	0.4.5	0.9.1+	1.1.2+	1.4.6+	1.7.1	1.8.2-	1.8.1	1.6.6	1.4.2	1.0.5	0.8.5	0.5.0	0.2.3+	0.0.5+	
24"		0.1.5	0.6.2-	0.10.4	1.2.2-	1.4.7-	1.6.1	1.6.0+	1.4.5-	1.1.6	0.10.2	0.6.5-	0.3.4+	0.1.4		
27"		0.0.5	0.0.5	0.3.2+	0.7.0	0.10.0	0.11.6-	0.11.4-	0.9.7	0.7.3-	0.4.5-	0.2.3-	0.0.5			

OFFSETS IN FEET, INCHES, & EIGHTHS, AS TO OUTSIDE OF CARVEL PLANK. PLUS & MINUS SIGNS INDICATE BIAS, NOT NECESSARILY EVEN SIXTEENTHS.

OFFSETS IN GENERAL ARE ACCURATE TO WITHIN A SIXTEENTH; FULL SCALE PATTERNS ARE UNRELIABLE DUE TO SHRINKING AND STRETCHING OF PAPER, & QUALIFIED LOFTSMEN SHOULD REPEAT SUCH WORK.

DESIGN #218
SPONSORED BY BOATING

6

AN OCEAN-GOING
ROWBOAT PROJECT

Ocean-crossing in rowboats is about as hard, or as easy, to justify as mountain-climbing or some other sports and exploits involving danger and hardship. It seems to me that anybody has a perfect right to undertake such things, without any qualifications, for money, or glory, or personal satisfaction. I would do no more to protect the ignorant and neurotic than to *try* to confront them with hard figures and to *advise* them to experiment alongshore, and to rescue them if asked and if the attempt at rescue did not involve much hazard, expense, or inconvenience.

Working out a boat for the purpose is an interesting technical exercise. I find it troubling that by definition you exclude a proven device, the sail, that would allow the supposed goal to be accomplished more quickly, easily, and safely, without losing your dependence on the wind or effecting any overall economy. However, this kind of definitive restriction is built into most sports; they're not widely thought of as disreputable. I think perhaps they ought to be, as an addiction to rule-cheating can be bad for the soul, but I don't want to show more fanaticism about it than I can help, and the problem happens to be related to a type of rowing that I do think is certainly ethical.

Whether a one-man or two-man boat works out better on paper for such a trip depends on dubious assumptions about power and resistance. A plausible case can be made for the one-man boat on such grounds, but the psychological case seems to me to be overwhelming, as with two people in trouble and danger, at least one of them will have his worries multiplied by responsibility for the other, and by trying to guess at the unspoken feelings and wishes of the other.

Eight pounds of food and water per day was assumed to be adequate, and one hundred days as the time to be allowed. Sketching the boat as she might float at each end of such a period, I found the length of twenty feet seemed about the least which would allow a good flow of water around the displacement involved. A flat midsection produced the least change of flotation from loaded to light, and also seemed likely to have the most comfortable motion. I suppose the hull as shown would pound badly in a head sea when light, but little progress can be made in such conditions in any case. This seems to be one of the few cases in which a sharp stern is better as well as prettier than a round or square one, as at the speeds considered it should make no appreciable eddies even when the deck goes under a wave crest. The low ends reduce weight overall and where it helps most, and, more important, reduce the windage. With the ends of the hull down in the water boundary layer, there is almost no tendency to blow off course.

The construction indicated is bent-frame carvel, but strip-planking would be as good and probably cheaper, while cold-molded plywood would be used if the budget could run to it. Smooth-skin construction would be preferred to lapped by being easier to keep clean. The best antifouling paint would be used, and it was planned to clean her bottom at sea from time to time with a brush on a line around the hull. She is as clean in shape as possible; I hope, judging by the behavior of the slimmer but otherwise similar *Kotick,* that she can get by without any fin, but if she has to have one after trial it would be a short, sharp-edged metal one six or seven inches deep at the extreme after end of the light load waterline. It's my fond hope that a man in really good condition in general, and in the hands and buttocks in particular, could keep this hull, in loaded condition, moving at three nautical miles per hour, forty-five minutes in each hour, sixteen hours a day. Allowing an average of one day a week total loss for bad conditions, three thousand miles are possible in the one hundred days normal supply duration, which corresponds roughly to the longest passage contemplated, that from the Canary Islands to the West Indies. This would be the last long passage; by the time it came up, the capabilities of boat and oarsman ought to be well established. The trip was supposed to start from New York, with increasingly long jumps to Chatham on Cape Cod, to Halifax or thereabouts, to St. Johns, Newfoundland, where a final decision would be made on the ocean crossing. The crossing would be to Ireland with such small help as the Gulf Stream might furnish, or to the Azores. I favored the latter as being much shorter and likely to be calmer; using meridian altitudes and a line of latitude I would think Flores could be found with reasonable certainty, let alone the larger and higher islands. Thence you would have what would by that time seem a routine pull to Lisbon, south to Gibraltar and the decision on whether to attempt to complete the round trip.

Three knots in a heavy boat suggests a short stroke with comparatively short oars, eight foot as indicated. This is just as well, as I would want at least two pairs each of spare oars and rowlocks stowed inside the boat and not out in the open causing wind and wave drag and deteriorating in the sun and salt. The seat has a deep cushion and a short slide, the latter not

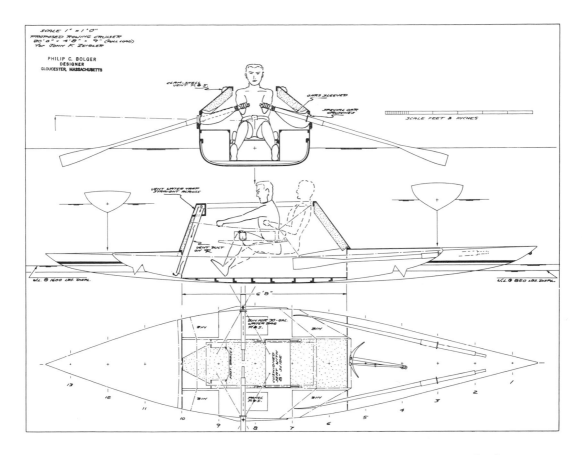

so much to increase the power of the stroke as to keep the legs exercised. It can be lifted off its track to make space to lie down comfortably on an air mattress. A heavy fabric cover can be snapped down over the top when the weather is too bad to row; ventilation with spray-trapping is provided; and there's height enough to sit up on the mattress. I meant to have one or more deadlights to see out when battened down, but did not get around to deciding just where they should go.

To ride out the gales she is bound to encounter in so much time at sea, she is supposed to rely on a sea anchor composed of planks lashed across the flukes of her regular anchor, streamed to a pennant on an eye in the stem for least chance of chafe. With the cockpit cover well lashed, she is reasonably watertight overall, and the high central enclosure gives her a good range of stability. I meant to have some handholds low down at the sides, inside, to enable the man to help her right herself if she landed bottom up after a breaking sea passed. As a last resort she has positive buoyancy indicated, so placed as to bring her right-side-up if swamped.

Various other details were contemplated in passing. The one I would work at hardest if I had to continue this design would be the method of shipping the oars. As sketched, the advantage of the low placement with tight sleeves is obvious, but it has the makings of a clumsy and irritating nuisance as well. They can be allowed to trail in position much of the non-rowing time in good weather, but I would think it important to work out some reasonably quick and safe method of bringing them inboard before completing the design. One sees some promising approaches, but the design was not carried to a point where I had a clear idea of just what I wanted done about it.

I have to admit to being rather taken with this design, which would be strikingly handsome to look at. (She should be painted white all over for least sun damage.) Preferring my own company to that of most other people's, most of the time, I'm not bothered by the fact that she can't be rowed with a second person on board. I do think I would like her much better if she was modified for much shorter, coastwise, cruising. If she could be planned for six or seven hundred pounds less weight of supplies, a considerable improvement in her model would be possible, and it seems to me that a cruising rowboat has some possibilities for week-ending and vacationing that are worth thinking about, for real pleasure in the doing as well as in the accomplishment.

7

ON ROWING

Twenty years or so ago the National Geographic Society sponsored an expedition to investigate a meteor crater down back of beyond in Labrador. The crater lake was to be sounded, so they took along a canoe, and, naturally, an outboard motor to drive the canoe. How else? That motor was flown at fabulous expense to the vicinity, and packed miles across nightmarish boulder terrain and down the precipitous wall of the crater with hardship and hazard complained of in the official account of the expedition. After arriving at the water's edge, I suppose they spent a half hour hooking it up and pulling on the starting cord before they sputtered bravely out to the middle of the lake, which was all of a mile and a half in diameter, took their soundings, and proceeded to reverse the whole process till the motor arrived in good order back in Montreal. Being careful men, I expect that they also took some paddles along in case the motor broke down.

Apart from illustrating that well-regarded scientists don't necessarily have any sense, this piece of lunacy is only an exaggerated example of a very common tendency. There are actually thousands of people using motors (and sails, for that matter) to do jobs that could be done quicker and easier, to say nothing of cheaper, with oars. Almost while I was writing this I saw a television ad for an electric outboard motor, guaranteed not to wake up your neighbors when you go fishing early in the morning; the thought is appreciated, but anybody could row the boat faster and farther, still in silence, than that motor could drive it.

I'm a great admirer of modern outboard motors, I should say; I've owned several and used them a lot, but the way some people use them is like trying to do your shopping by airplane when the market is in walking distance, not because you like flying so much, but because you don't realize that it's possible to walk. Even disregarding cost, it's folly to insist on a motor for very short distances because the trouble of bringing the motor to the starting point is out of all proportion to any that it saves when ready. Motors

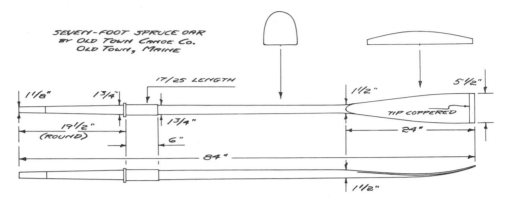

Figure 1

enable a boat to make headway against swift streams or gale winds, or to cover a long distance quickly, or to keep very heavy loads moving reliably; they're not needed or efficient for short distances, light loads, and pleasant weather, and in particular they're not sensible when the thing sought is recreation for a given *time,* rather than arrival over a certain distance.

The very fast rowing boats developed for racing and race-training are not good for casual recreation because they're too fragile and slow-turning to take into crowded places and narrow inlets, or to launch and beach on most shores. Their seating is too inflexible to be pleasant for many hours at a time, and, although the decked types are surprisingly good in rough water, for other reasons they need a more alert crew than seems good to me for a carefree excursion. On the other hand, the stubby and shapeless dinghies of the common type are about as good as anything for enjoying a small and smooth anchorage but limit the range severely. In the earlier chapters I've presented several intermediate types and commented on their capabilities and limitations.

With the designs there are some recommendations on oar lengths. I've never been able to work out a satisfactory formula for this because freeboard comes into it as well as breadth; I have to diagram it by trial and error, trying to arrive at proportions that enable the oar handles to just clear each other at the boat centerline with oars horizontal and eight twenty-fifths of the oar length inboard of the lock. In boats very high out of water, you have to settle for some overlap of handles on the recovery or the handles will be too far apart on the stroke; in very low boats some separation of the handles on recovery does no harm. Generally speaking, a good deal less than twice the spread of the locks will serve, and I'd prefer to have oars a little short of the ideal than much too long.

For the design of the oars themselves, the same kind of considerations come up as in selecting a boat. The perfect oar for straightforward rowing

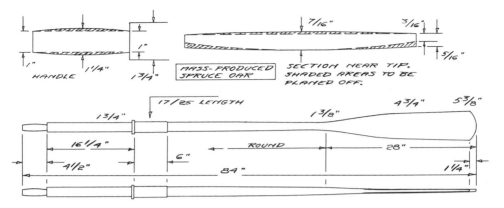

Figure 2

is too fragile in the blade to stand use as a pole on shallow bottom, or the banging against rocks that is bound to happen sometimes when you have to cramp close up against a bank to avoid a foul stream. Figure 1 is a drawing of an oar made by the Old Town Canoe Company of Old Town, Maine; it's one I've used for many years and never seen improved for clear-water rowing, but it's a little weak in the blade for rough treatment and has become very expensive on account of the complex shape. Figure 2 is an ordinary mass-production oar generally available either in ash or spruce. For pleasure rowing the ash version is no pleasure; the spruce oar is plenty strong and stiff, and not terribly worse to use than the Old Town if you shave one side of the blade a little, as diagrammed, and take off the foolish swell in the handles with a spoke-shave to make them less prone to blister your palms. Any serious rowboat should have two pairs of oars (and row-locks; a friend of mind nearly blew away toward Portugal once when he broke one of his only pair of locks offshore) and it seems good to me to have one pair of each type.

I think a very good oar could be made along the lines of the Kotick paddle shown with that design, but I haven't gotten around to trying a pair. The spoon shape I don't think is at all crucial though no doubt it's more helpful in an oar than a paddle.

With cheap oars there's a lot to be said for using them bare and replacing them when they begin to develop a wasp-waist from wear at the locks. A protective wrapping of fiberglass and resin might also be a good device though I haven't tried it or seen it tried. I've tried about everything else I can think of for protection and found nothing much better all around than the traditional leathers, which stand up pretty well if given some lanolin now and then, and when worked-in have about the right kind of surface. The soft and sticky rubber sleeves have much too much friction and tend to walk the oar inboard stroke by stroke in the most exasperating

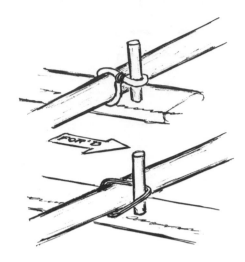

Figure 3

way when used with the common type of rowlock. The slick, hard, plastic collars are so slippery that it's almost impossible to hold the oar at the selected place in the lock; they do work very well if the button or other stop is placed exactly right and is the right size and shape for the lock.

The oldest type of rowlock is the single thole-pin with a slack lashing around the loom, described in the account of the battle of Salamis in *The Persians* of Aeschylus, who was there; this arrangement is still common in the Mediterranean and is a good one (see Figure 3). The main drawback is that the lashing tends to bind and prevent the oar from being laid in or removed from the pin quickly, especially when several turns of light twine are used instead of a single loop of hard rope with a seizing between oar and pin. The arrangement on the same principal in which the oar is given a shoulder with a hole for the pin is slightly better this way but is more likely to break the pin. The North River rowlocks often seen, in which the oar pivots on a horizontal pin between horns, I haven't used much but think rather well of despite having been brought up to sneer at them because you can't feather the oar; a softwood oar used with them needs some reinforcement in way of the pin or it will break there sooner or later.

Figure 4 shows a slight modification of the standard bronze rowlock, in case somebody should feel like making his own, or a manufacturer should think of improving the design. The only alteration is the change in the inside shape from a circular arc to part of an oblong, to stop the oar from riding up the front of the lock as it takes the thrust of the stroke—a small nicety that wouldn't complicate manufacturing in any way. Figure 5 is a more drastic modification, copied from a British design I once saw. This has the advantage of the thole pin type in that the bearing of the oar doesn't swing around appreciably with the stroke and stand out of position through

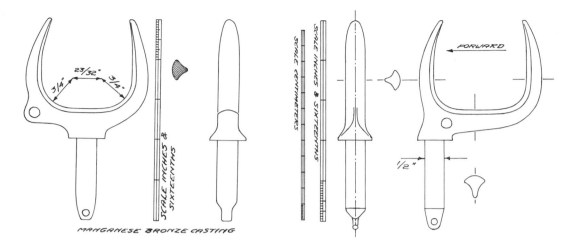

MANGANESE BRONZE CASTING

SCALE INCHES & SIXTEENTHS

SCALE CENTIMETERS

SCALE INCHES & SIXTEENTHS

FORWARD

Figure 4   Figure 5

the recovery, which is the reason for the oar tending to walk inboard in the usual type of lock. The oar can be laid in further without taking it out of the lock, and isn't restricted in how far it can be laid in as with double thole pins, which have to be much too far apart for convenience in other respects for this reason. On the other hand, there's no difficulty about taking the oar out of the lock and no undue friction if you choose to feather. A lock like this will punish an unleathered oar much less than the usual symmetrical rowlock. This particular design will fit the standard half-inch sockets and the trial pair were substituted for the original pair in my Thomaston Galley. The movable seat in the Galley made the slightly different relationship of oars and socket position no problem, but in a rowboat with fixed thwarts there would probably be enough margin in the exact placement of one's bottom on the thwart to take care of the difference of slightly over an inch. These locks are available from Erik A. R. Ronnberg, Jr., 2 Summer St., Rockport, Massachusetts 01966, for the time being.

When you start out for a row, resist the urge to start fast. Paddle gently away, preferably down wind. If the wind shifts you can have it with you both ways; if it holds you'll feel stronger to buck it later. Row with the arms only for the first few hundred yards, only very gradually starting to put your back into it. The shorter the oars you're using, the shorter the stroke must be to make efficient use of your strength. A full reach of the arms and swing of the back won't pay with oars under about seven feet at least, and a sliding seat won't pay with oars much under nine feet long, though there's a case to be made for it with shorter ones for keeping up good circulation in the legs.

After half or three-quarters of an hour of gentle rowing, say a mile and a half or so in good conditions, it's time to start stepping up the stroke. I find about twenty-five strokes per minute a good pace to maintain once I'm warmed up, for a two- or three-hour pull without a break. That much rowing will blister most peoples hands somewhere. As far as I know, nothing will harden the hands except habitual rowing; pushing a lawn-mower or using tools of some kind ought to help, but it seems that every kind of use leaves a soft place somewhere. Gloves or bandages are not help-ful. Opening the hands on each recovery does help and for this reason as well as the wear and tear on the wrists I never feather my oars except when trying to look elegant for a short distance. The only real reason for feather-ing is to avoid catching the unfeathered blade in a crest and raising a cloud of spray to blow over you; in the very low-sided racing-type boats you must feather when there's any amount of chop because you can't raise the blade clear of the ordinary crest and must drag it through, which is a good reason for avoiding the use of such extreme boats. If you plan on feathering much of the time, have the oars looser in the locks than is otherwise best, and use slippery leathers, or none.

The best way to avoid blisters on a long row is to take a break about fifteen minutes out of each hour, or, much better, to have two oarsmen row-ing alternately; done this way, six or eight hours of rowing will leave no scars at all on hands even slightly hardened. A particular case of a man and wife who take turns of forty and twenty minutes respectively may be sug-gestive. Bucking a strong wind and sea for a short distance (and there is no future in doing it for a long one) they both pull together, to get over the hard place quickly, but pulling double isn't economical of energy under ordinary circumstances unless you practice it so much that you can keep time completely automatically.

Backaches developed while rowing are usually caused by pulling round-shouldered. If you snap your shoulders back straight whenever you think of it, and now and then grip a wrist behind your back and strain the shoulders back, an erect posture becomes habitual and may just avoid back troubles from things other than rowing. Various other stiffnesses com-plained of have been known to yield to slight adjustments in the height of the seat, position and angle of foot braces, or even something as small as learning to look over your shoulder out of the extreme corner of your eye and not trying to see further around than dead ahead on one turn of the head. Rowing is a more complicated skill, to do well, than it looks, and it's easy to develop bad habits from solitary practice, as for instance I have an ingrained habit of hooking my thumb over the end of the handle of the oar, acquired from years of use of oars slightly too short for the boat. A girl who had rowed a lot in rough water had acquired the habit of "rowing over stumps," digging the oar deep and raising it high, and was wasting more energy than she realized in waving the blade of the oar up and down, at times when there was no need of it.

I've written in the previous section about a scheme for a rowing exploit, and in the ordinary way there's a strong tendency to try for impressive distances and speeds. I do it too. "Had a nice pull around the Cape the other day," I say casually, alluding to a seventeen-nautical-mile circuit. The intention, as far as it's any more than pure showing off, is to convey that if I, who don't look very athletic, can do that (and I have, several times) almost anybody can row a lot farther than they realize. Nevertheless, that's not really the way to enjoy rowing, and it's not what rowboats are better at than power or sailboats. What the rowboat is ideal for is extracting the maximum enjoyment from a small area and for getting behind the scenes. You can't very well follow an America's Cup race in a rowing boat, but in a pretty one, now that such are rare, you can prowl around under the stern overhang of a moored cup candidate and have her famous skipper come back to talk with you instead of sending a hard-faced crewman to drive you away as would happen if you tried it in a motorboat. When somebody tells you that such and such a narrow creek just goes to the town dump, you can go and look, and find that by pushing on through a culvert beyond the dump you come to a lovely isolated glade in a patch of woods, full of bird calls and with a clear brook splashing down into the end of the creek over a series of small waterfalls. Reservoirs and semi-private water, where any other type of intrusion won't be tolerated, are available to the oarsman implicitly or explicitly because he is trusted not to disturb his surroundings; on the other hand, he may picnic in shade and quiet among the supporting piles of a warehouse built over a commercial waterfront because his lack of fear of entanglement and incentive to examine closely every inch of shores he would whisk past in a powerboat led him to the possibility.

8

THOMASTON GALLEY

15'6" x 4'1"

Harold Payson was building light dories, for pleasure rowing, to my designs, and had the usual pile of letters asking for some arrangement to put outboard motors on them. I brushed them off for awhile, saying it was impractical and would spoil a good pulling boat and make a slow and dangerous outboard, but eventually he said that if I didn't come up with a better idea he would put motor wells in some of the dories. He knew that would really make me think about his problem.

The obvious thing to do is to make a dory type wider on the bottom and carry the breadth all the way back. So you get buoyancy and stability aft where the weight is apt to be, and enough stability all along so that the motor doesn't take her feet out from under her when you swing it to steer, as happens in proper dories. I've done many boats like that, and eventually did one for Harold, the Sea Hawk Skiff design later on in this book. This makes a decent outboard motorboat, but not one that is a pleasure to row, especially with any great load aboard.

It seemed to me that some deadrise would have to be used to combine enough stability to be reasonably safe and comfortable with the motor in use, and a clean bottom to row pleasantly. With plywood planking specified, that meant a long bow overhang if a hard knuckle in the forefoot was to be avoided. I thought about sneak boxes, where this problem is solved by making the hull very low and building up the sides and ends in way of the cockpit. Eventually it struck me that there was no need to cut down the stern, that in fact if it was built up into a sort of quarterdeck it would produce just that extra buoyancy that was needed to carry the motor, and moreover the combination of low bow and high stern would balance her up in windage and stop the bow from blowing off as it does in most rowing boats. It was at this point, looking at the ram forward and quarterdeck aft, that I began to call the design the Galley.

About that point I also noticed that I had the makings of a fair sailboat

The Galley under sail and oars

hull, if I could introduce a rig and some lateral plane without cluttering it up too much. Hence the third drawing and a complete three-way combination boat, but very peculiar to look at.

Harold took his courage in both hands and built one. That was four or five years ago at this writing, and nobody could claim that the design is a great success as a commercial proposition, there being perhaps a dozen or so of them in all. But Harold still uses his, which he keeps on a mooring and uses exclusively for sailing, and I still use mine, which lives on a light trailer in my garage and is used almost entirely for rowing (though I sail it now and then when I have a long way to go or when conditions are perfect), and we're both extremely fond of the boats.

Rowing, I find I average about three and a half miles per hour in good conditions for two hours or so; I think I can spurt five and a half for a short distance because I can get through a local canal against the strength of the tidal stream, alleged to be five knots, without much trouble. By starting in the morning calm, rowing, and sailing when the wind came up, I've more than once covered twenty-five miles or so in a day.

My sail was made by an awning maker and one of Ted Hood's men once intimated he thought he could improve on it for windward work; she certainly is not very close-winded and the trouble is not due to making much leeway with the single leeboard either to windward or leeward. As may be, she feels lively and spirited, with a very good positive sensitivity on the tiller and ideal balance. I don't value any possible improvement enough to pay for a better sail, myself.

I once borrowed a 3 h.p. outboard motor, recalling briefly that that was the original idea. She was just ordinary, as far as I could see, except that it was nice to prove that, as calculated, two men could lean over the stern and

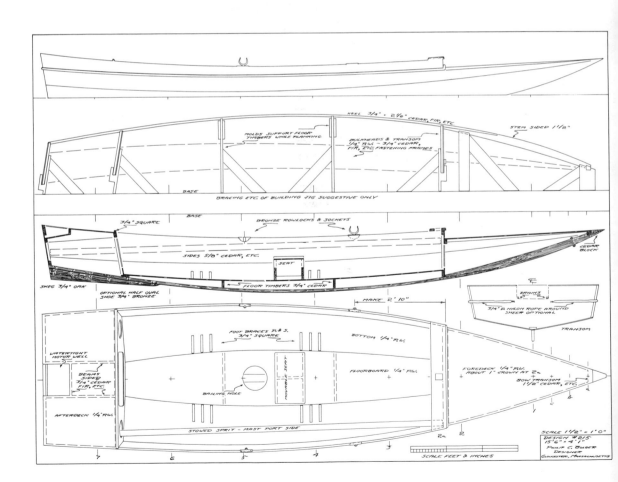

reach the propeller without using up the buoyancy of her big stern. A couple of the other boats are used for marsh gunning and seem good at it, quiet and easy to camouflage, and roomier inside than most. As to this last point, the movable rowing seat (idea by L. Francis Herreshoff) makes plenty of room to lie down and the sail neatly covers the open part with the sprit for a ridgepole (also lifted from L.F.H.), but I find I've lost most of my early enthusiasm for camping out in the New England climate in open boats.

No problems with the construction have developed in several years of frequent use, including any fair day in winter in my case and one time in particular having to drag the boat across an ice floe that had blocked the way home. The boat is noticeably flexible under sail, the thrust of the leeboard twisting the side in and out in the puffs, but there doesn't seem to be any harm in it. I haven't had a chance to sail one with the optional plywood sides, which are somewhat lighter and, some think, easier to build, but I presume there is little difference in behavior. The Galley weighs around

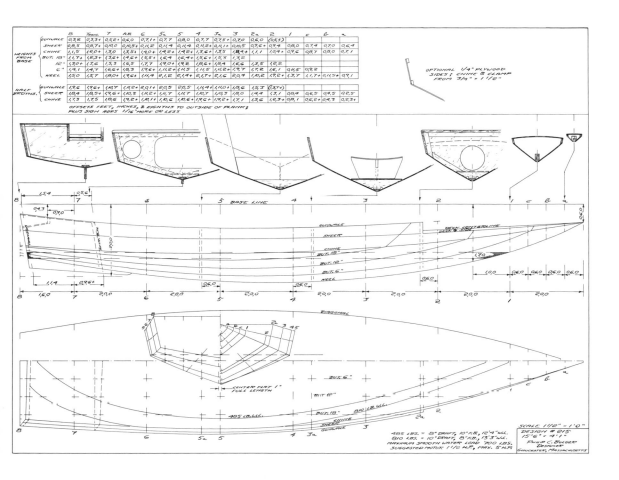

A buoyancy demonstration

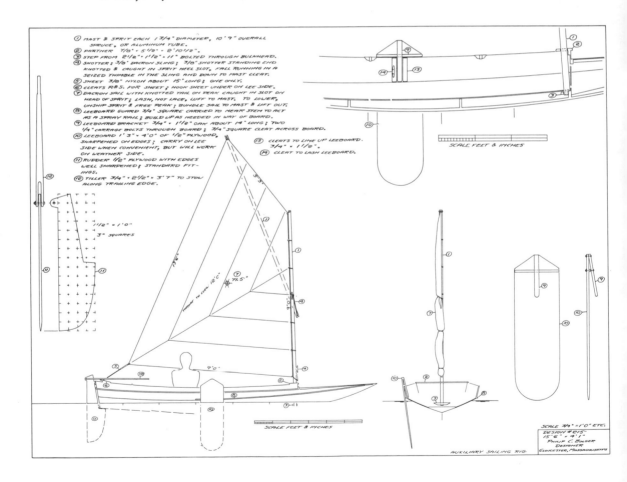

140 pounds stripped, and mine has around thirty pounds of gear normally carried, including the rig, rudder, leeboard, spare oars, anchor and rode, bailer, and life jackets. The long snout makes her very easy and quick to haul up on the trailer without wetting the wheels, and I must say I feel smug watching the agonies that the people next to me on the launching ramp go through.

She is intended strictly for protected water, of course; by trimming her by the stern she can go through or over a tolerable chop without much trouble under sail or power, but rowing her to windward in open water is a wet and nasty business I take pains to avoid; I keep a light dory for such work, and for when I feel like playing with surf, but in smooth water the Galley rows as well in a calm and better in a breeze, and is otherwise more comfortable. If nothing else, having enough stability to stand up and look around without doing a trapeze act is frequently convenient.

I admit to being quite proud of this design; apart from being the only successful attempt at a row-sail-motor combination I ever came across, it tends to blow up a designer's vanity when an unusual solution to a troublesome problem works out exactly as expected.

9

DOLPHIN

18'0" x 4'0"

At the time I was discussing the *Victoria* design with the editors of *Boating,* I mentioned that by stretching the proposal out a little, a nice peapod or miniature whaleboat could be produced. They decided that the transom-stern boat would be better under average conditions and that the extra length would make it seem, if not be, too big for a great many people. Some time later I decided to go ahead and draw it up anyway as a compan-ion piece to *Victoria.* They have almost exactly the same midsection, but the sharp-stern boat is longer and heavier, with higher ends. She could use the same construction, but for variety's sake I drew her as a strip boat. As designed she is suitable for rougher water, greater loads, and rougher treatment. She ought to be a first-class surfboat pulling four oars, but a man in the habit of rowing alone would find her too heavy, and showing too much windage, to be ideal for his purpose.

All the same, she isn't nearly as big as she looks in plan form, her low sides and general proportions being deceptive when there's no human figure to give scale. The displacements marked on the body plan are significant; since the hull as designed, with normal equipment, will certainly run to four hundred pounds and quite easily more, two people would be her capacity on the designed line. She would still be competent in moderately rough water with four, or five if some are not heavyweights, but not more. She is not meant to pull six oars at a time, the three pairs of locks being intended to give more flexibility in loading her. The sharp stern, with its easy line right up to the gunwale, is helpful this way; you don't have to be as careful not to trim her by the stern as in a square-stern boat, and it will help her keep her way in a chop when deeply loaded.

I'm very dubious about the sailing rig. I drew it up with great care to see how it would go, knowing there would be demand for it as there always is with a pretty rowing boat. The sail itself is good enough, and the drawings show that the spars can be stowed more or less out from under foot if

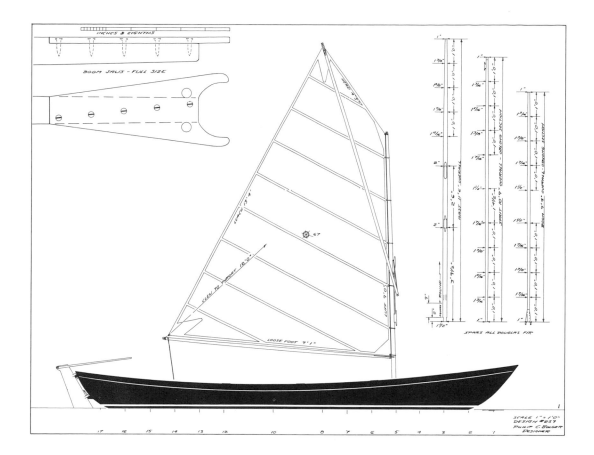

some pains are devoted to the racks. But I'm sure that centerboard is smaller than it should be, in spite of putting more hours than I'd care to guess at into thinking about it. Between trying not to cut the structure up too much, and not to castrate one of the oarsmen or break his fingers, and still arrange the pennant so that the opening in the case can't flood her in a crisis, I nearly gave up on it. It may be I should have done so, especially as I think the resistance of the slot in the bottom will be quite noticeable when rowing. I don't think anybody will row far without being reminded to pull the board up, however, as when down it will have perhaps half as much drag as all the rest of the hull. I leave it on the plans because she undoubtedly will sail tolerably with it and is in any case not going to stay alongside any Lightnings or other real sailboats, but, if I was to build one of these, I certainly would have one or another of the forms of leeboards shown elsewhere in this book.

I did think of giving her a long shallow keel such as peapods often had, six inches average depth or so, below the rabbet. It's an attractive idea, giving great stiffness to a hull and protection in grounding and hauling up,

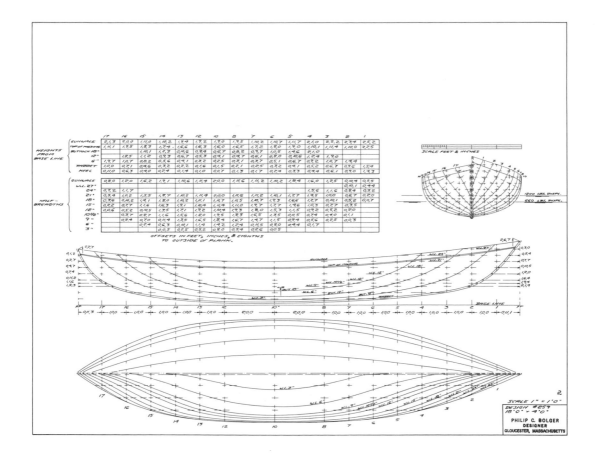

cheap and simple to build, and making no excrescences inside the boat; I've once or twice been tempted to try such a keel, for those reasons, on my Thomaston Galley. However, it would be out of sight but not out of mind, when rowing. An experiment of rowing the Galley with rudder and lee-board in place convinced me that, though the drag of the keel might be less than the deeper appendages, it would be plenty to take all the pleasure out of rowing her. Besides, it would probably be even less effective for sailing than the undersize centerboard. A deeper fin keel would be the end of her as a beaching or practical trailering proposition, of course. As with other auxiliary rowing boats, you can make some sacrifices in sailing ability and still have a useful and enjoyable performance, but the moment you make the least concession that works against the rowing, you've lost her as a pleasant rowing boat; even the extra length, high ends, and strong construction introduced into this design to make her good in rough water have put her close to the line where she will cease to be much satisfaction for a single oarsman to take his exercise in.

For a group of children on their own, she might come into her own.

They might not appreciate her beauty, though they would remember it later and live with a high standard in consequence, but in one way and another she would keep them busy, and once they had had some practice with her they could be turned loose to take her where they liked without supervision. As long as they kept some grasp of the fundamentals and were warned about places where the surf or breaking reefs could be really dangerous, they could be reckless and short-sighted in a boat of this kind and still survive to benefit by the experience. Unfortunately, she's an expensive affair to try on a group that probably yearns for a fast motorboat instead, but there may be camps and clubs that could make a project of several of them, and it's sometimes possible to awaken the snobbery of the oarsman even in quite young people.

KEY TO CONSTRUCTION

1. Keel, stem, sternpost double ¾″ plywood, sawn out with butts staggered about as shown.

2. Planking ½″ soft pine or cedar; garboard strakes about 3½″ wide amidships with seam on centerline; rest of planking in about 1″ wide strips, rift grain as far as possible, edge-nailed on three-inch-plus centers with galvanized wire nails about 2″ long or more; resorcinol or epoxy glue, or a high-grade elastic seam compound, applied to the seams as the strips are laid; a few strips may be tapered or feathered off to keep the lay on the molds easy, or, for a nice appearance, to bring the upper strips parallel with the gunwale.

3. Cap and shoe ¾″ x 1½″ mahogany or oak, bevelled to a ¾″ face.

4. Gunwale stringer ½″ x 1″ mahogany.

5. Breasthooks ¼″ plywood.

6. Thwart webs ¼″ plywood with ½″ mahogany or fir fastening frames.

7. Thwarts, and fore and stern sheets, ¼″ plywood; thwarts have ½″ x 1½″ beams across forward edges.

8. Bilge stringers sided ¾″ mahogany or fir; may be laminated or sawn out of about 7″ wide plank, to finish molded about 2″.

9. Gunwale knees are part of web frames, shaped about as shown and by trial to form racks for mast, boom, sprit, and one pair of oars.

10. Oarlock blocks, fir or mahogany, shaped to fit against and under gunwale stringers #4, from blocks about 1″ x 2″ x 8″; rowlocks any of the larger standard types.

11. Three stretchers or foot braces 1¼″ diameter mahogany or fir, squared to fit about ¾″ slots in the bilge stringers or sister keelsons #8; if centerboard is used, fit stretchers each side of case, with a notched cleat to take their inboard ends on the case.

12. Foam buoyancy under foresheet and sternsheet may be expanded or cut from blocks; if the latter, they should be well fitted and tightly packed as the foam is meant to support the thin flats as well as provide positive buoyancy.

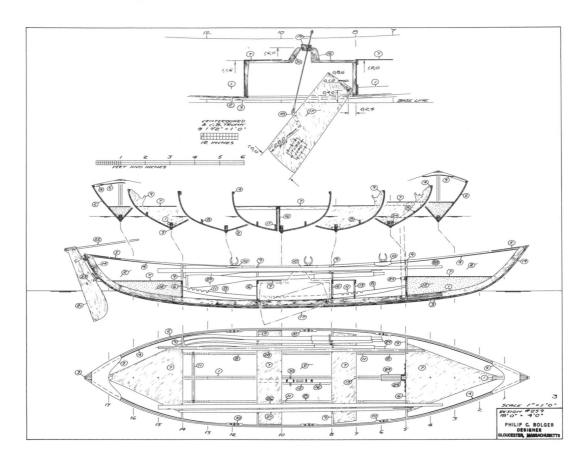

13. Post ½″ x 1″ mahogany or fir, on centerline tongued into keel; if no centerboard is installed, another one on the second thwart.

14. Half-inch wide hole through stem and stern to take painter and stern line with a stopper knot inside.

15. Fastening piece on outside of centerboard case from ¾″ x 2½″ fir or mahogany.

16. Centerboard case sides ½″ plywood; headblocks and top spacers sided ¾″, molded about as shown, all glued up.

17. Centerboard ½″ plywood with outside edges sharpened to slightly blunted edges. ½″ diameter by 5″ bronze carriage bolt pivot pin; lead insert about as shown.

18. Bronze or stainless steel straps ⅛″ x 1″ x 6″ let flush into centerboard and riveted; ⅜″ diameter pennant pin.

19. Pennant ¼″ nylon; stopper knot on end; pennant runs in a tight hole in a softwood block shaped to plug opening in top of case.

20. Trim moldings (see offsets for location) ¼″ x ½″ mahogany.

21. Rudder blade ½″ plywood, about 3′ 2″ overall, 9¼″ maximum width, shaped about as shown; note how tiller can swing over to stow along back of blade.

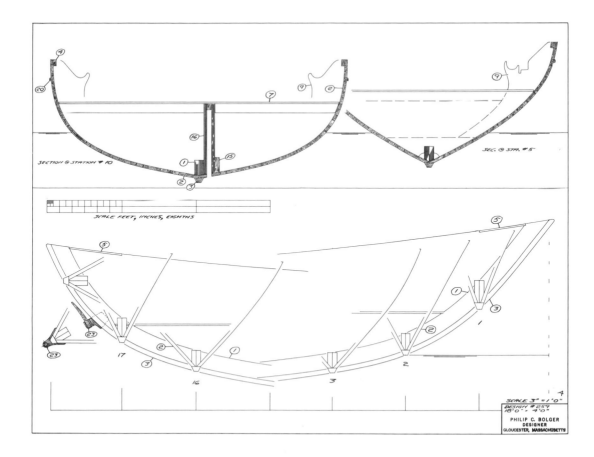

22. Tiller ¾″ x 2½″ mahogany, about 3′ 0″ overall, tapered to ¾″ square at hand end; ⅛″ x ¾″ x 6″ straps to ¼″ pivot bolt.

23. Cast bronze pintles and gudgeons; the long and curved lower pintle, and probably all of these fittings, will have to be cast specially from new patterns taken from the hull.

24. Mast step cheeks molded ¾″, sided about 2″, overall length about 14″ mahogany, fir, or plywood, bolted or riveted through keel; the step itself is just cut out of the top of the keel.

25. Mast partner a galvanized or stainless steel strap ¼″ x 1½″ x 18″ (before bending) bolted through the web or bulkhead; round off edges that might score the mast.

26. Fir or spruce mast; see sail plan for suggested dimensions.

27. Fir boom with ¼″ plywood jaw.

28. Fir or spruce sprit.

29. Three pairs of spruce oars; shown 8′ but actually 7′ 6″ is suggested; at least one pair should be straight-blade type rather than the spoons shown, for poling and other rough use.

30. Oak or ash pin about ½″ x 5″ for centerboard pennant.

10

GLOUCESTER YAWL

21'0" x 5'6"

A young man came to me with a scheme to take groups of boys out in small boats, for sport and the betterment of their physical and mental health. He had been connected with an established project of the kind, but thought that smaller groups in more and lighter boats would be an improvement. He thought four boys and a councilor would be about right for each boat; this would allow the boats to be light enough for beach cruising, not too heavy to row a good distance, and, it was to be hoped, of a type that could be built in high school manual training shops. He proposed to build the prototype himself.

Generally speaking, I tend to distrust missionary types, but this project was much to my taste, and I agreed to contribute a design, only exacting an understanding that the prototype was definitely to be built, no question of it being a pipe dream.

Thinking hard about the requirements and potentialities for awhile, I came up with a sketch version of these plans you see. The owner, who had expected a sloop-rigged dory, was naturally somewhat startled, but I suppose my explanation sounded erudite, and he was anxious to get on with it, so in the end he was a little impatient when I explained that it would take at least three weeks to get out the working plans.

When I did hand over the working drawings, these here printed, he showed them to a number of people for comment, including a very distinguished yacht designer, and they one and all told him that the design was a disastrously bad one, would be slow and clumsy and would quickly break up. They also told him that Bolger was notoriously irresponsible; wild ideas like this, they told him, were what you got if you didn't hold his nose tightly down on some safe and sane standard. Thinking this over for awhile, he came in to me and explained that he had discovered my incompetence and duplicity and would, of course, not build from the design, but that he was willing to let me design him a dory type to a strict specification

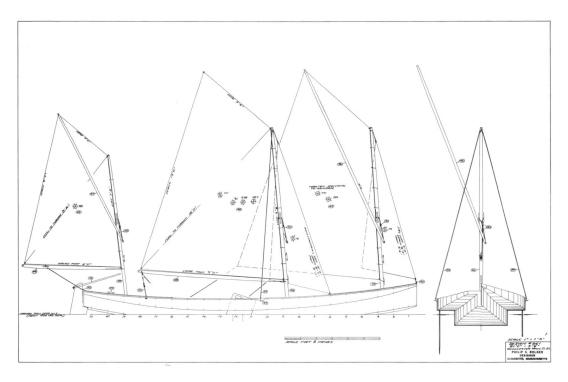

by his informal committee of experts. If not he would build a Seabright skiff design he had found in one of Howard Chapelle's books. I'm afraid I was malicious enough not to try to tell him what reputation *those* have with boatbuilders not brought up on them.

The moral of all this I take to be: don't trust anybody with pretensions to moral superiority.

As for the design, I'm very sorry it wasn't built. I had beautiful visions of it booming along, three or four in company, in a strong quartering wind, and then stealing up some creek in line ahead with imaginary horned helmets by the steerboard; also of my jigsaw puzzle of bits and pieces turning suddenly into a boat before your eyes in a high school shop with many hands.

What was supposed to be accomplished was a design that could be built by house-carpenter types without the guidance of a skilled loftsman with a minimum chance of losing the intended shape, and capable of being duplicated very quickly once the patterns had been established and proven. It should be fast with four oarsmen, and not helpless with one; lively to sail with crews varying in numbers and experience; light and shallow enough to be beached; roomy enough for five people to sprawl around in, or even sleep in at a pinch; and having enough buoyancy and reserve stability to be taken alongshore in open water without having the consequences of carelessness become lethal.

It's an old observation that sharpies suffer from being wide for their length, and from having flaring sides. My flow theory accounts for this, but I've long thought that a sponson sharpie would produce the benefits of a flaring side without the drawbacks, or most of them. In this case it was especially attractive because it allowed so much flat area for sitting and lying down, and it eliminated most of the tricky bevels that make dories so much harder to build than they look. The gunwale does not go under with the treacherous ease of the flared-side boat, and though the wetted surface jumps sharply among waves or when heeled, you don't, on paper at least, create the problems with eddy-making that flared sides do. It's easy to see how this boat could be made faster, but I see no way to do it without making it somewhat less roomy and a great deal more difficult and laborious to build. In any case, I was confident that the boats would sail and row well enough to keep the boys interested. (I should say that I would on no account use a model like this for a real cruiser because it would be intolerably noisy, full of great bumps and crashes underway in a seaway, and talking all the time in a rippled anchorage. In a beaching boat, this isn't an overriding defect as I see it.)

As for the structure and its alleged weakness, the critics of course looked at the midsection and thought it would collapse downward at the internal angle, the one marked #8. I much doubt they contemplated the extreme rigidity of a 3/8″ plywood beam 9″ deep, held in a curve rigidly at the bottom and with a substantial flange at the top, with an unsupported length of only ten feet: the upper sides. However, it's true that the arrangement is rather heavily dependent on good gluing and well-driven screws, which you might find had not been produced under the circumstances, and I'd planned on testing the strength as soon as the assembly was finished by having several men stand on the gunwales and bounce up and down with increasing force. If loud cracking sounds began to make themselves heard, we could substitute a solid bulkhead and thwart for the midships rowing seat, and that would be that. But I hoped to get by as shown because an all-clear arrangement is an order of magnitude more pleasant to live with than a cut-up one, even when the divisions are quite low.

I think it was primarily the rig that frightened people not well enough up on history to recognize it as reactionary rather than experimental. I had in mind the rigs of eighteenth-century three-mast luggers and beach yawls (hence the name-tag of the design), though I chose spritsails rather than dipping and standing lugs, for, among other reasons, the shorter masts. All the spars are easily taken down and stowed inside the boat out of the way of the oarsmen. All can be made of stock lumberyard fir. No expensive fittings are needed, and the sails themselves can be made flat by any awning-maker and still work pretty well. The weight and drive of the whole rig is low to the water for least capsizing effect, yet the aerodynamics are by no means crude and the area is considerable for the weight it has to drive. Area for area, the rig is no doubt "inefficient," but it's very large and powerful for its cost and the boat can carry it in winds that would knock her over if the masts were taller, so I should say it is quite efficient in a slightly different sense.

All these odd sails also give everybody something to do, but, if she has to be sailed short-handed, just one or two of the sails can be used, and will be adequate since she'd be in light condition. The way the rig is supposed to be handled is outlined in the specifications.

What they say about me has this much truth: I do love unusual and extreme boats, and I was tickled at the thought of the outrage the design would cause and how it would be silenced when she was tried. I got the black eye without the vindication due to my missionary not thinking of keeping his word. Of course, anybody who is thinking of building one now might do well to bear in mind the odd chance that the Very Distinguished Yacht Designer was right about her. I don't think he was, and I haven't had any more failures than he has, but the prospective builder will have to judge for himself, it being his work and money.

KEY TO PLANS AND ASSEMBLY ORDER

1. Hull bottom in three sections of ½″ plywood.
2. Bottom butt straps ½″ x 6″ plywood. (Assemble bottom sheets flat on floor, securing to butt straps with glue and ¾″ #7 screws or with clinch nails. With bottom inverted, i.e., with butt straps underneath, block up center of bottom about 15″ above ends and secure chine logs around edges with glue and clamps, then 1″ screws.)
3. Chine logs ¾″ square fir or other reasonably hard wood of good gluing properties, such as mahogany. (Mark bottom centerline on outside of bottom, and parallel lines for edges of bottom shoe.)
4. Bottom shoe from 1½″ square fir, etc., beveled to ¾″ on bottom edge; if full length is not available, scarph toward ends as shown, not near the middle. (Turn bottom right-side-up and align bottom shoe under it; block up ends about 15″ above center and glue and screw or nail bottom down onto shoe. The bottom should now hold its approximate designed rocker without forcing.)
5. Lower sides ⅜″ plywood with ⅜″ x 6″ butt straps; assemble flat, using ½″ #6 screws well countersunk, or clinch nails, at butts.
6. Stem ¾″ x 1½″ fir, etc.; glue and screw to one side and bevel before assembly of sides. (Spring lower sides around bottom, placing blocks supporting bottom in such a way as to bring lower edges of sides flush with underside of bottom; secure with glue and ¾″ screws or with nails.)
7. Transom ¾″ fir, etc., a vertical piece the full height, and sponson arms attached by a 12″ backing strap; see dimensions sheet; cut for stringers before installing, but check bevels against actual assembly. (Set vertical part of transom

in place and fasten sides to it. If sides now in place tend to fall inboard amidships, put in some casual bracing to hold them nearly plumb to bottom.)

8. Inboard sponson stringers ¾″ square fir, etc. (Spring these around inside lower sides, starting against the stem; clamp, glue, and screw to sides.)

9. Sponson bottom ⅜″ plywood with ⅜″ x 6″ butt straps. (Assemble sponson bottom flat on floor; better clamp a couple of temporary braces across the two sides to make sure it isn't distorted in handling. Place on top of lower sides and spring down on to them; line up with inner edge of inboard sponson stringers and screw and glue down in place.)

10. Outboard sponson stringers ¾″ square; clamp, glue, and screw to outer edges of sponson bottoms.

11. For'd and after bulkheads ⅜″ plywood, without openings; fastening frame all around ¾″ x 1½″ fir, etc. (Put upper arms of transom in place; install the two bulkheads at their marks on the bottom, or anyway as near to the marks as will fit neatly; glue and screw all solidly in place.)

12. Upper sides ⅜″ plywood with ⅜″ x 6″ butt straps. (Assemble flat and spring around outside sponson bottoms, keeping lower edge flush with bottoms; make sure these sides stand close to plumb through the middle part of the hull where they're not supported at their top edges.)

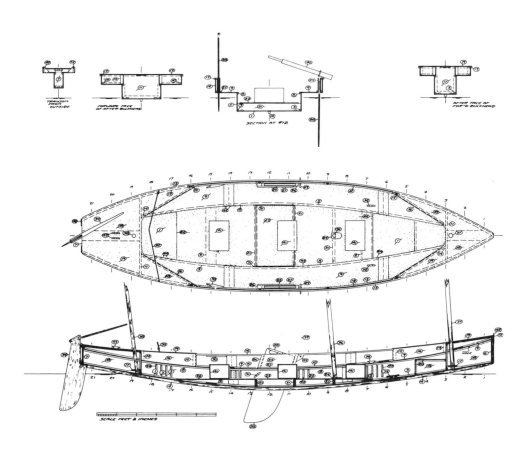

13.   Inner and outer gunwale stringers bent on to edges of upper sides, the inside ones first; start at stern, noting that one inner stringer laps by the other at the bow. Use ¾″ screws from side into inner stringer, 1½″ screws or nails, countersunk, from outside stringer into side and inner stringer.

14.   Vertical posts from 1½″ square fir, etc., screwed and glued to bulkheads, bevelled to take quarter webs.

15.   Fastening cleats from ¾″ x 1½″ on sides to take outboard ends of quarter webs.

16.   Quarter webs ⅜″ plywood with ¾″ square fastening frames top and bottom. Pick up accurate patterns for these from the assembled hull. Secure them very solidly, making sure there are no holidays in the glue by slobbering, as they will be very heavily stressed when sailing hard or if people jump up and down on both gunwales at once.

17.   Mast steps ¾″ x 5½″ x 5½″ fir, etc., or (better) scrap plywood ½″ or thicker, mounted on two 1½″ square fore-and-aft pieces as shown on construction profile; cut hole to suit shape of masts to be used; heel rests on hull bottom, without tenons, though heel of mizzen might well be bevelled off as shown.

18.   The ends of the hull, including the spaces walled off by the quarter webs and the bow seat, are to be filled with foam buoyancy, which may be either low-pressure expanding foam or cut blocks; in either case make sure there is clear space left to step the masts either by shaping the blocks or by plugging against the expansion. Take care also that these spaces have small openings at all low

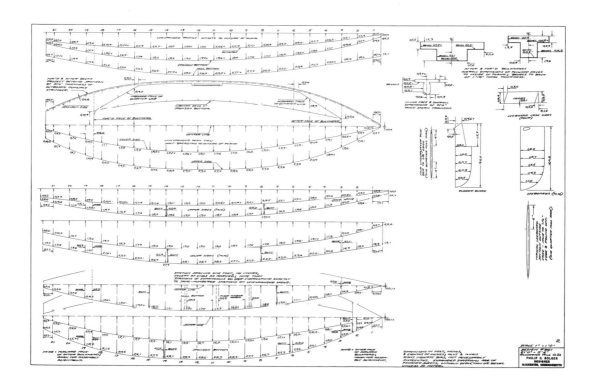

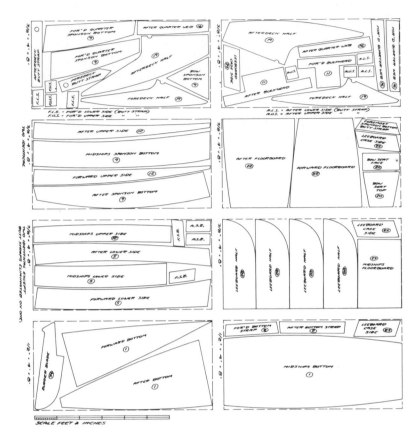

points to let off condensation water; there will naturally be no leakage, so the water must be from condensation.

19. Forward and after decks ⅜″ plywood with ⅜″ x 6″ butt straps on center-line where shown and nowhere else. Pick up patterns for these from the assembled hull. Make sure they are well and truly glued and screwed or nailed to the gunwale stringers, bulkheads, and quarter webs, as they're the main tension support for the sponsons.

20. Bow seat ⅜″ plywood.

21. Floor timbers sided about 1½″ fir, etc.; the two deep ones amidships are molded about 4¼″, the one under the mainmast about 3″; 1½″ screws from bottom plus glue. Note locating marks for these on bottom assembly. Cut drain limber holes under these timbers well out to the sides.

22. Fixed floorboards ⅜″ plywood, screwed down to cleats on lower sides and to floor timbers; space under them filled with expanding or block foam.

23. Removable floorboard section ⅜″ plywood; space beneath kept clear at sides for bailing. Stow anchor (15-pound Yachtsman-type suggested) and at least 200 feet of ⅜″ nylon rode near centerline.

24. Mainmast step cut from ¾″ fir or scrap plywood, screwed and glued to floorboard.

25. Leeboard case sides ⅜″ plywood (on the sheet-use diagram, one of the

four of these is on a ½″ sheet; put this one on one of the inboard faces in hopes that will be the side somebody kicks).

26.   Leeboard case headblocks 1″ x 1½″ fir, etc.

27.   Cleat ¾″ square (or bigger if handy) glued and screwed to case sides before assembly on headblocks; glue down and drive some 1″ screws or nail up from the outside of the sponson bottoms. (Glue and screw leeboard cases to inside of upper sides over precut slot; shim up rather carefully to get a watertight joint with lower sponson stringer.)

28.   Leeboards double ⅜″ plywood; i.e., to finish ¾″; ¾″ plywood could be used if handy at some saving of labor but with loss of the built-in fairing centerline of the double construction. Fair the boards about as shown to their edges as they may vibrate if left square or bluntly rounded; fit with handhold at top with ¾″ square handle which also serves to keep them from dropping through; drill holes in boards and cases and furnish pins on lanyards to keep the boards from floating up; other holes in boards only to hold them in various raised positions.

29.   Belaying pin, wood or metal, each side for mainmast shrouds; ¾″ padding inside and out about as shown to give the pins a solid bury.

30.   Foresail sheet hooks port and starboard ¾″ fir, etc., bolted through sides; these sheets should never be made fast so no cleat is shown.

31.   Five-inch cleat port and starboard for mainstaysail sheet.

32.   Five-inch cleat port and starboard for jib sheet.

33.   Eight-inch cleat, bolted through hull bottom, for fall of mainstaysail tack pennant. This cleat is the entire forward support for the mast, so make sure it is solid; two ¼″ bolts ought to be plenty.

34.   Rudder blade ½″ plywood; standard pintles and gudgeons. Note that, as designed, rudder can only come off if swung 90 degrees. Tiller from 1″ x 2¼″ x 3′ 1″ mahogany tapered to about ¾″ oblong at hand end; ¼″ bolt to rudder; tiller stows along back of blade.

35.   Main sheet horse ½″ nylon or manila; one end held with a stopper knot under hole in outside gunwale stringer, other end with a snap hook to engage a loop through the stringer on the other side.

36.   Mainmast 12′ 0″ overall; 2½″ diameter to within about 3′ of the top, thence tapered to about 1½″ diameter. May be a hollow box spar if preferred, or an aluminum tube, in which cases it needs no taper except for looks. If solid, it can be Douglas fir, or spruce, or about anything handy, and it would probably be a long time before it gave any trouble if it was of less diameter than specified.

37.   Foremast 11′ 6″ overall, otherwise same as mainmast; if it's tubular or otherwise hollow, plug to above deck level.

38.   Mizzen mast 10′ 0″ overall, 2″ diameter tapered to 1″ at top from about 4′ below the top.

39.   Main shrouds ½″ dacron or manila; stopper knots through holes near masthead; belay to pins #29.

40.   Ten-foot two-handed oars, four plus one or more spares; stock type or special design, or a mix. Stock oars, especially if ash, will be much stronger for

poling, fending-off, etc. but very heavy and badly balanced.

41.   Rowing seats to be portable; suggest ¼″ plywood boxes with hinged lids for personal stowage, water bags, or whatever; folding camp stools would be more comfortable and easy to stow; bedding rolls might do if tightly packed and lashed. If somebody wants to get really ingenious, it would be fairly easy to arrange these seats to slide on a central track to give more power in rowing and some exercise to the legs.

42.   Stem plate 1/16″ x 1″ x 6″ with hole for snap hook on tack of jib. Also ½″ plywood fairleads for mizzen sheets screwed to outside of transom.

43.   Two five-inch cleats for mizzen sheets.

44.   Foot braces ¾″ square on lower sides.

45.   Sails all a lightweight dacron; sailmaker to decide cut; if suitable-weave cloth is available, designer would like to see all of them cut old-style with cloths parallel to the leaches, or better still, miter-cut with the lower cloths parallel to the foot. The heads of the three spritsails and the luffs of the two staysails should be very strongly roped, especially the luff of the main staysail which could stand to be wire.

No halyards: the luffs of the spritsails are lashed to their masts; not laced, but with separate lashings. Head pennants of staysails pass through holes near mastheads and stopper-knotted there.

46.   Fore and main sprit 12′ 0″ overall, about 2″ diameter for the middle six feet, tapered out to about 1″ diameter at each end. Hole at each end for peak outhaul and snotter; cleat for outhaul about where shown.

47.   Mizzen sprit 9′ 0″ overall, about 1½″ diameter through the middle four feet, tapered to about ⅞″ each end; end holes as above.

48.   Main boom 9′ 2″ not including jaw; ¾″ fir plank (or heavier to 1″ if handy) molded 2½″ the middle four feet, tapered out to 1½″ each end; jaw ¼″ (or ⅜″) x 3″ x 12″ plywood. Sheet ⅜″ nylon with a snaphook to the horse, through a light block to the hand; better not belay it.

49.   Mizzen boom 6′ 2″ not including jaw; ¾″ plank molded 2½″ at the biggest place about 1′ 6″ from clew end; taper to 1½″ each end; jaw same as main; separate ¼″ sheets port and starboard to control twist.

50.   Snotters all ⅜″ dacron about 5′ long; stopper knot on one end holds against hole in foot of sprit; other end whipped. Snotter slings the same, spliced around masts and large, smooth thimbles; cleats on masts about as shown.

Rigging and sailing procedure

Set mainmast upright in step; belay tack rope of staysail to cleat #33; set up shrouds tight to pins #29 with mast as nearly plumb as possible. Pass peak outhaul through hole in head of sprit and belay to cleat on sprit after hauling out as far as it will go. Pass whipped end of snotter through hole in foot of sprit, thence through thimble in snotter sling, and haul out till head of sail is taut, belaying to mast cleat; set up snotter now and then when sailing to take out the stretch, as the sail will set badly and the boat not point well if the peak is allowed to sag. Boat will sail well with mainsail and mainstaysail, and for shorthanded maneuvering the staysail may be bundled up and stopped.

To set other sails, set mizzen next, or first of all if setting all sail on at anchor. Step foremast last, and better stop up the jib before stepping the mast if there's weight in the wind; break out jib when underway.

Alternately, the boat will sail and handle well with mizzen and foresail only, with or without jib. This would be a good rig when frequent changes from oars to sails and back are needed, as the mainmast obstructs one of the oar positions. It may be mentioned that while the jib and staysail are not powerful sails in themselves, they will, if properly set and sheeted, much increase the power of the two large spritsails.

11

ROSE PINNACE

28'0" x 6'6"

This big pulling boat was part of the design of the 18th-century-style full-rigged ship *Rose* and was proportioned to fit an open space on the starboard side of that vessel's deck. The boat rows well; two men can keep her moving respectably, and, with six good men pulling hard, she seems to go very fast.

The strong flare of the bow made her a hard boat to plank up; it was adopted because it was thought she would be likely to be towed in a seaway, but it also does make her somewhat drier in a head sea under oars, and gives a better position for the foremost oarlocks. A flatter sheer and wall-sided bow would row faster, though less comfortably and safely, in a head wind.

The stern is not as pretty as the wine-glass type, but having tried both I'm of the opinion that the flat skeg has less drag and tracks better in a following sea, besides being easier to frame and plank.

The transom was designed to take a sizable outboard motor, perhaps ten horsepower. With that much power she should go seven or eight knots into a fair breeze. Three horsepower would drive her at a good rate of speed in a flat calm. With a twenty-five horse motor she would stand up on end, make great sheets of spray, and probably show several kinds of instability. An inboard engine would completely ruin her for rowing, of course, but I must say I think she would make quite a good low-powered utility with some of the thwarts removed and the skeg deepened to swing a good-sized wheel.

As for the rig, it was designed mainly to be easy to set up and stow, and to lie down inside the boat without being intolerably in the way. It's a fast rig reaching in strong winds, but slow before the wind and usually not very close-winded. The lack of booms makes it an excellent rough water rig. However, its behavior is secondary as it's strictly auxiliary to the oars, meant to be used for long runs when rowing becomes a bore. The point is that of all rigs it has the shortest and lightest masts without rigging, hence the least hesitation and delay in setting it up or stowing it. If these,

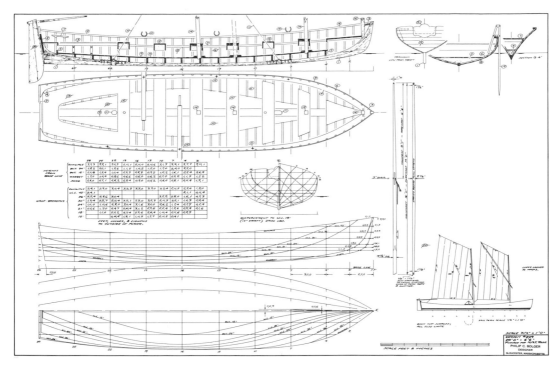

or taller, masts were left standing their wind resistance would be of the same order as all the rest of the boat with seated crew; what's more, at four or five knots in a dead calm the air resistance of a standing mast is quite noticeable to the oarsmen.

In the same category is the single leeboard, which can be instantly shipped; this board has no ballast and will need to be held or lashed against floating up. It works as well on the windward side as to leeward if the boat can be kept from heeling too much. The rudder shown is meant for sailing and there really ought to be another one of much smaller and shallower blade design for steering under oars, as the deep rudder has much drag under oars. It's important to bear in mind the minute power a rowing boat has: this one has three horsepower by the most generous estimate I've ever seen, and probably no more than about half of one horsepower, sustained, though of course the "torque" is quite large by comparison. Working with such tiny powers, tiny resistances become very important, as to both wind and water.

KEY TO PLAN

1. Keel:, stem, skeg all sided 2½″ hardwood.
2. Transom 1½″ softwood, edge-drifted without any frame except cleats at sides to avoid end-grain fastenings.

3. Breasthook 1½" hardwood.

4. Shelf sawn and scarphed from 1½" hardwood, sprung to sheer profile; place in molds before framing and notch for frame heads as shown.

5. Floor timbers 1½" hardwood bolted through keel.

6. Frames steam-bent oak about ⅞" x 1½".

7. Thwart stringers ¾" x 1½" hardwood.

8. Planking ⅝" hardwood or ¾" softwood; bronze screw fastened.

9. Center floorboard screwed down on every floor timber; ¾" x 7½".

10. Outer floorboards removable.

11. Hoisting straps ⅜" x 2"; two ¾" bolts each through keel plus screws as shown; to take ⅝" (three-ton) forged steel screw pin shackles.

12. Thwarts 1" x 12", with ¾" x 6" faces; fill in under with urethane foam buoyancy.

13. Stern seats ¾" plywood.

14. Mast steps reinforced with 1½" hardwood pads; third (middle) step is for sailing with one sail instead of reefing.

15. Rowlocks for 15' spruce oars, six in all, plus two or more spares.

16. Bitt 3½" square hardwood bolted through stem and breasthook.

17. Hardwood cavil-cleats.

18. Rudder blade about 1¼"; tiller to swing over and stow along trailing edge.

19. Leeboard (one only) 1½" x 2' 0" hardwood with bolted cleats and arm as shown to hook over either gunwale (will work on weather as well as lee side). Notch shelf slightly and provide socket (not shown) inside to prevent fore-and-aft movement.

20. Rig: spars spruce or fir; sprits are same length as masts, one 16' 0" and one 14' 0" each. No halyards; sails are lashed to masts. To lower, start snotter; pull end of snotter out of slot in foot of sprit; lower peak and pull peak rope knot out of slot at head of sprit; bundle sail up to mast; lift out mast and sail and stow along centerline. One ½" sheet for each sail, say 15' long for mainsail and 12' for foresail; provide cavil-cleats like #17 each side for foresail sheet. No blocks; ½" snotters run in big thimbles siezed in mast slings.

21. Plug for motor cut-out 1⅝" softwood with ¼" plywood facing inside and out.

12

YELLOW LEAF

15′6″ x 3′0″

Just back from Buzzards Bay, they have an annual race to celebrate some occasion or other. The competitors go in pairs, and the course leads over land, across some ponds and creeks, and through swampy land; some of the water is always too deep to wade; some of the land is always dry and rough, but according to the wetness of the season the condition of the swamp varies. I understand the course can be anything from three-quarters able to float a boat to three-quarters carrying it. The boats are supposed to be home-built.

You see the problems: the boats have to be light enough to be carried some distance at a run; they have to float two husky people; they should be fast when propelled by paddles or oars; the less water they draw when loaded, the more of the swampy part can be paddled; and the shape ought to be suitable to being skidded over mud. Incidentally, the spirit of the home-built rule should be observed by keeping to a design that can be run up in a day or two without more exotic materials than can be found at the town hardware store.

The design turns out to be quite graceful. A punt with about foot-wide transoms at each end would probably be a little faster paddling in smooth water, but it would be heavier to carry and take longer to build, so the pretty pointy shape is no sacrifice to style. It needs at least as much sheer as shown so it can be launched end-on down a reasonably steep bank.

To save the last ounce of weight the structure is designed to be flimsy and flexible. The gunwales will weave in and out, the bottom can be felt to bulge where you step, and as soon as the resin gets brittle in the chine tape, some heavy-footed type will stamp the bottom out getting into her. Regarded as a substitute for a canoe rather than as a one-shot racing machine, that chine certainly ought to be beefed up; the obvious way to do it would be by means of a conventional chine log, say a half-inch square. But this would add perhaps four pounds to the all-up weight. You may remember one of Bill Mauldin's greatest cartoons: Willie and Joe are

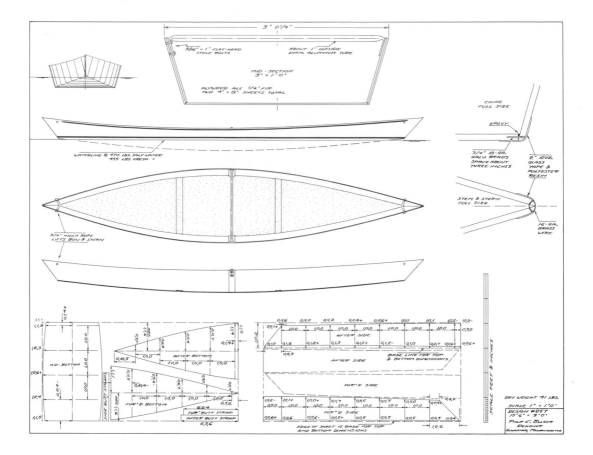

trudging down a long, long highway loaded with the components of a heavy machine gun among other things; old Willie says: "Ya wouldn't get tired if ya didn't carry extra weight. Throw the Joker outa ya deck of cards." Of course if you hop in with both feet in the heat of the race, and the bottom of the boat pops off there and then, you might figure that the chine logs, or knees, or whatever you decide to put in, are more like the gun than the Joker, i.e., worth carrying along.

I think perhaps the best way to make the boat stronger would be to use five or six layers of glass tape, inside and out, instead of the single one shown. A very strong joint can be made by the scheme Eric Tasker invented; in this the plywood is not in contact; you set it up leaving about a three-eighths-inch gap, put a layer of tape on one side over the gap, fill the space with a chopped-glass and resin slurry, and tape over while the slurry is still soft. A layer of four-inch tape and a reinforcement of two-inch on the outside and the same inside makes a strong job; I built a dinghy by this method which stood all kinds of banging around for ten years or more and has still not given out though some cracks are starting to show. The trouble with the method from a point of view of this design here is that you have to jig it up some way to hold the plywood in position while you get the tape and slurry on. On the other hand it's the incompetent's friend, because nothing has to fit, the size of the gap not being important.

As may be, you could add reinforcement enough to double the designed weight and still be lighter, to say nothing of cheaper, than a plastic canoe of equal capacity.

13
KOTICK

15'0" x 1'11"

I wanted this canoe to use in places without launching ramps; she's light enough to pick off a car rack and carry to the water on my shoulder. This and the convenience of not having a trailer tagging behind the car seem to me to be the advantages of a canoe; once you get afloat a good rowing boat has the better of it most ways. I'd certainly go to a rowing boat rather than try to make a two-seat kayak; His and Her kayaks would make more sense, retaining the slenderness and short length that keeps the weight in *Kotick's* case under forty pounds.

Her length seems to be about right for recreational paddling. A longer hull, or one fuller towards the ends, could be spurted faster; if I really put my back into it as hard as I can for a hundred yards or so, the stern waves begin to lap across the deck at the stern in this one; six miles an hour or so, I suppose. But she's good to paddle a long way at a gentle pace and little affected by wind or small waves. A shorter hull would be quicker-turning on a slalom course but would waste a lot of energy zig-zagging; even with *Kotick,* I had to practice a little before I could keep her straight subconsciously. She's no more than average breadth for her type, but not tricky because of the flat-bottomed, hard-bilged midsection suited to her intended speed. I should say that I never set foot in her, or any such boat, without a life jacket on, as it seems to me it could spoil one's entire day to get bottom-up in one with a lost or broken paddle; I'm in no hurry to join the short list of boat designers drowned in or out of craft of their own devising.

I use a cushion of 4" foam rubber about 15" square, without a cover. It's very comfortable for up to three hours or so, and has friction enough to make the foot brace shown unnecessary. A back cushion doesn't seem to add much, and it's my impression that she's a little happier trimmed with her bow high as the photo shows. I don't ordinarily go into rough or fast water, and for motorboat wakes and such the comparatively high coaming

Kotick *is lightweight*

Kotick *at moderate speed, beginning to settle aft*

and the trunk over my toes keeps the water out of her well enough. The skirt shown, brought loosely up around the chest, is mostly to collect the inevitable drip from the paddle, plus insurance; it's not a pretty thing, but is a lot cooler in summer than anything closer-fitting.

If I can find a float, or a good solid stake within arms reach of navigable water, I'm very happy when I want to get in or out, though I'm still just limber enough to be able to sit in the boat out of shallow water and then double my legs in after. Much more comfortable is being able to step gently in with both feet, squat down onto the cushion, and slide the legs ahead off the floorboard, but for that you need something to steady yourself if your balance is no better than mine.

The strip construction keeps my mind easier about skim ice and drift-wood than stretched fabric, however good sealskin may be. It's not much heavier, though a lot more laborious to build. Harold Payson made a winter-evening project of *Kotick* and charged me a lot less than such a beautiful job of work should be worth, but as designed she's really only suitable for a good woodworker to build for himself as a hobby project. As you see, she is a beautiful thing to bring out of your cellar into the sunlight, the one catch being that from then on the owner is deathly afraid she

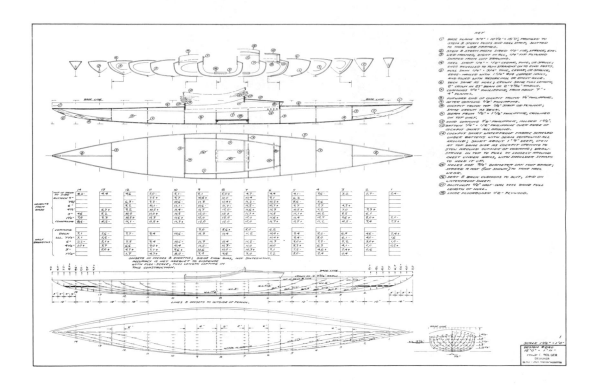

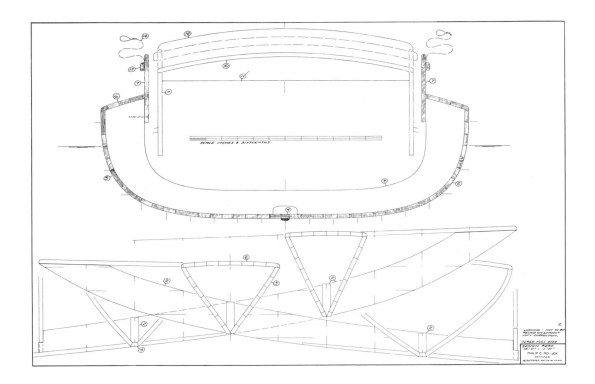

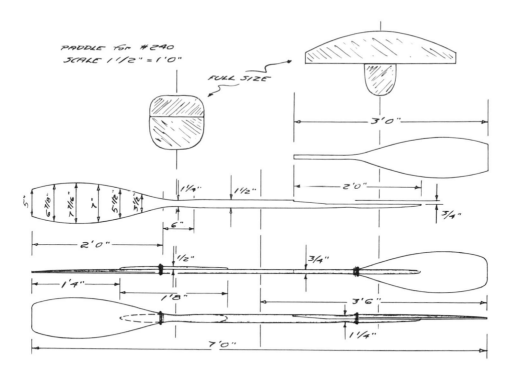

PADDLE for #240
SCALE 1 1/2" = 1'0"

FULL SIZE

will get dropped and broken. I was never quite happy about carrying her around 'till I'd persuaded Edey & Duff down in Mattapoisett to pull a mold off her so she could be duplicated economically in case of accidents.

The paddle shown in the rather rough drawing is a great success. It was made of two planks of white cedar and is extremely light, yet it's apparently strong enough. I use left-hand control and have had no problems with the unsymmetrical grips. The big flat blades don't seem to have any drawbacks, in wind or otherwise. The drip moldings are quarter-inch manila rope spliced around, with tiny softwood wedges to fill in the gaps; they work pretty well, though sooner or later you always splash yourself somehow, hence the cockpit skirt.

I don't at the moment see anything I would do differently on this design, unless it would be to cut down the coaming slightly at the forward corners of the cockpit where it has now and then bumped my hands.

14

FIELDMOUSE

7'9" x 4'0"

I built the original *Fieldmouse* myself, to test the idea that a boat could be built to fit on an eight-by-four piece of the deck of a cruiser and still be lively enough to be fun. The result gave an impression of tremendous speed, with great boilings and roarings and most quick and sure handling in stays; she would even perform that trick in which you start the sheet slightly and hold the tiller over with your foot, when a good enough boat will go round and round indefinitely without moving the sheet or the tiller, tacking and jibing in a circle of twice her length or so; a pretty thing to see and useful if you need to keep the boat in a small space but under full control.

The square bow does not make her wet as the spray blows to leeward. It does have a tendency to dig in before the wind, but the boat is so dominated by crew weight that it's never a problem to hold it up. Raking it enough to make any difference would either put her over the stipulated eight feet, or shorten her waterline enough to hurt her performance.

Of course the real speed is very low. I suppose all those sound effects take place at about three knots; she has probably never sailed at four. But this is an advantage under some circumstances. If you feel the urge to sail but only have a small pond to sail on, the slower the boat is, the better, as long as she doesn't feel dead. *'Mouse* is almost excessively exciting at times, her sail plan being huge for her size and weight, and a fleet of them could cram more racing tactics into a puddle a hundred yards in diameter than the twelve-meters can find in Long Island Sound.

In reworking the original *'Mouse* design, I increased the displacement; the waterline marked, with end transoms just touching, is for 526 pounds; a man, a woman, and two small children would about do it, and she's so deep inside that the forward coaming is chest-high for a five-year-old. There are plenty of big cruisers with less comfortable cockpits than this one. As small dinghies go she is neither wet nor treacherous, though not, of course, to be recommended for rough-water work.

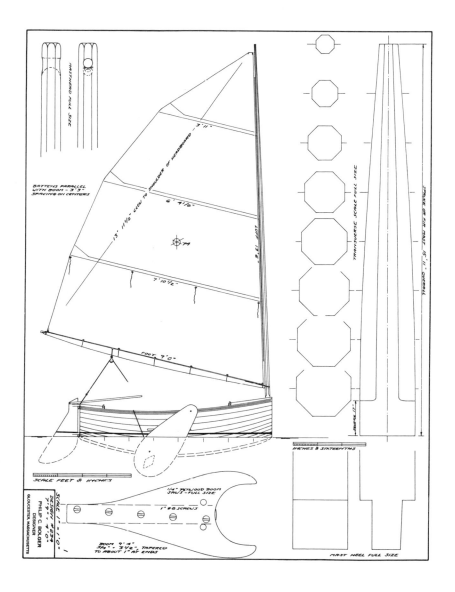

The original multi-chine
Fieldmouse

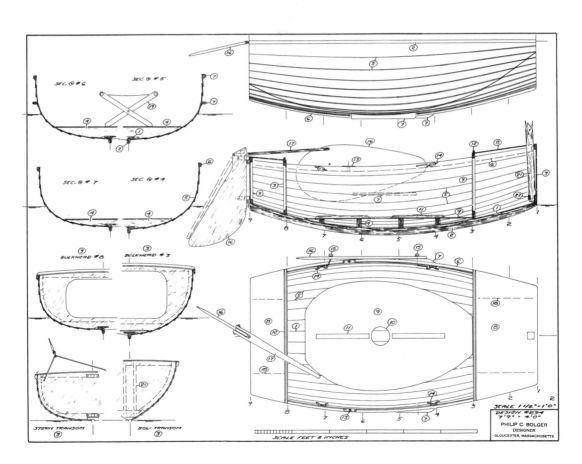

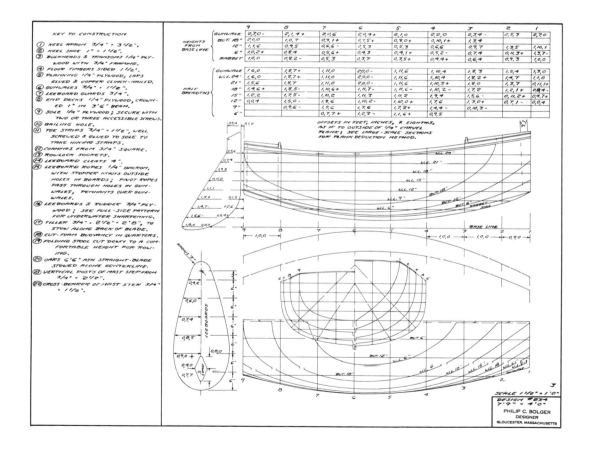

KEY TO CONSTRUCTION

1. KEEL APRON 3/4" × 3 1/2".
2. KEEL SHOE 1" × 1 1/2".
3. BULKHEADS & TRANSOMS 1/4" PLY- WOOD WITH 3/4" FRAMING.
4. FLOOR TIMBERS SIDED 1 1/2".
5. PLANKING 1/4" PLYWOOD, LAPS GLUED & COPPER CLINCH-NAILED.
6. GUNWALES 3/4" × 1 1/2".
7. LEEBOARD GUARDS 3/4".
8. END DECKS 1/4" PLYWOOD, CROWN- ED 1" IN 3'6" BEAM.
9. SOLE 1/4" PLYWOOD; SECURE WITH TWO OR THREE ACCESSIBLE SCREWS.
10. BAILING HOLE.
11. TOE STRIPS 3/4" × 1 1/2", WELL SCREWED & GLUED TO SOLE TO TAKE HIKING STRAPS.
12. THWARTS FROM 3/4" SQUARE.
13. ROWLOCK SOCKETS.
14. LEEBOARD CLEATS 4".
15. LEEBOARD ROPES 1/4" DACRON, WITH STOPPER KNOTS OUTSIDE HOLES IN BOARDS; PIVOT ROPES PASS THROUGH HOLES IN GUN- WALES, PENNANTS OVER GUN- WALES.
16. LEEBOARDS & RUDDER 3/4" PLY- WOOD; SEE FULL-SIZE PATTERN FOR UNDERWATER SHARPENING.
17. TILLER 3/4" × 2 1/2" × 2'8", TO STOW ALONG BACK OF BLADE.
18. CUT-FOAM BUOYANCY IN QUARTERS.
19. FOLDING STOOL CUT DOWN TO A COM- FORTABLE HEIGHT FOR ROW- ING.
20. OARS 6'6" ASH STRAIGHT-BLADE STOWED ALONG CENTERLINE.
21. VERTICAL POSTS OF MAST STEP FROM 3/4" × 2 1/2".
22. CROSS-BEARER OF MAST STEP 3/4" × 1 1/2".

		9	8	7	6	5	4	3	2	1
HEIGHTS FROM BASE LINE	GUNWALE	2.3.0 -	2.1.4 +	2.0.6	2.0.4 +	2.1.0	2.2.0	2.3.4 -	2.5.3	2.7.0
	BUT. 18"	2.0.0	1.10.7	0.9.1 +	0.7.5 +	0.8.0 +	0.10.1 +	1.3.4		
	12"	1.1.6	0.9.5	0.6.6 -	0.5.3	0.5.3	0.5.6	0.9.7	1.3.5	1.10.1
	6"	1.0.2 +	0.8.4	0.5.6 +	0.4.3	0.4.1 +	0.5.2 -	0.7.4	0.11.3 +	1.3.7 -
	RABBET	1.0.0	0.8.2 -	0.5.3	0.3.7	0.3.5 +	0.4.4 +	0.6.4	0.9.3	1.0.0
HALF BREADTHS	GUNWALE	1.6.0	1.8.7 +	1.11.0	2.0.0 -	1.11.6	1.10.4	1.8.3	1.5.4	1.3.0
	W.L. 24"	1.6.0	1.8.7 +	1.11.0	2.0.0 -	1.11.6	1.10.4	1.8.2 +	1.4.7	1.1.0
	21"	1.5.6	1.8.7	1.11.0	2.0.0 -	1.11.6	1.10.3 +	1.8.0	1.3.7	0.11.1 +
	18"	1.4.6 +	1.8.5 -	1.10.6 +	1.11.7 -	1.11.6 -	1.10.2 -	1.7.2	1.2.1 +	0.8.4 -
	15"	1.2.2	1.7.5 -	1.10.2	1.11.3	1.11.2	1.9.4	1.5.6 -	0.11.2 +	0.4.7 +
	12"	0.9.4	1.5.0 -	1.8.6	1.10.2 -	1.10.0 +	1.7.6	1.3.0 +	0.7.1 -	0.0.4
	9"		0.9.6 -	1.5.6	1.7.6	1.7.2 +	1.4.4 -	0.10.3 -		
	6"		0.7.6 -	1.2.7 -	1.1.6 +	0.9.5				

OFFSETS IN FEET, INCHES, & EIGHTHS, AS IF TO OUTSIDE OF 1/4" CARVEL PLANK; SEE LARGE-SCALE SECTIONS FOR PLANK DEDUCTION METHOD.

SCALE 1 1/2" = 1'0"
DESIGN #234
7'9" × 4'0"

PHILIP C. BOLGER
DESIGNER
GLOUCESTER, MASSACHUSETTS

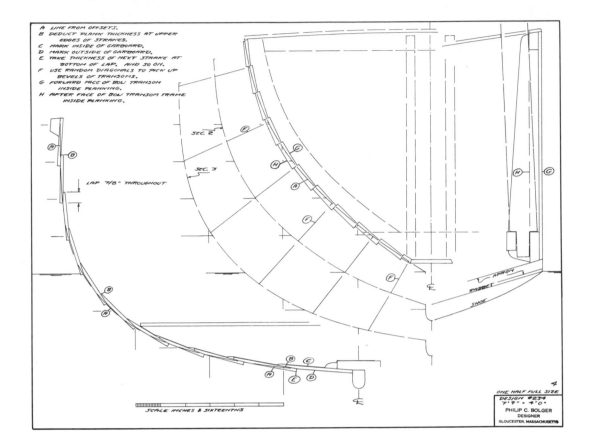

The leeboards are exactly as used, with satisfaction, in the first boat. They need much ballast and the inserts shown are minimal. The rope attachments as shown are cheap, simple, not liable to damage, easy to detach when stripping the boat, and they make it possible to pick the boards over the gunwale and dump them inside. The catch is that they leave the boards loose in all planes; running before the wind one or both boards will flip out off the hull and bounce along the surface. Then if you suddenly haul up on the wind or jibe, there is a disconcerting skid and jerk as the board brings up on its guard. The only time the boat capsized while I had her was on this account plus the fact that I hadn't gotten around to installing the foot braces.

She will weigh around seventy pounds stripped. Light weight is desirable for carrying her around on land; otherwise more weight is of no consequence, and almost any method of construction, except sheet plywood or metal, is suitable. The shape would not be economical in fiberglass as she wouldn't come out of a one-piece mold, which is why she is a better design than most production boats can be.

15

FEATHERWIND

15'6" x 4'6"

Around 1961 I let myself be talked into designing a sailing dory about this size. Even then I knew better, but a boatbuilder who was putting out rowing dories from a model of mine had a massive file of correspondence demanding a sailing version, and he was in a state of agony over the sales he thought he was losing. I widened the bottom and reduced the rake of the stern, filled out the curve of the ends in plan view, and worked in a heavy steel centerboard, all with a view to giving the tender and tippy dory some power to carry sail. When I came to try the boat, knowing what to expect of dories, I thought she was pretty good; she felt lively and went where she looked, and she could be kept on her feet if you paid close attention. The customers, however, as I should have known, were all ignorant of sailing dories except as a myth. They thought her tender and cramped, not as pretty as the rowing dory (which was true enough), and above all they were shocked at being asked to pay for the spars, sail, rudder, and centerboard.

This design here is what I ought to have done. This time I didn't spoil the boat trying to make it look like a dory; I drew the best flat-bottomed, straight-sided boat I could, to sail, the result being a light version of an old-time flat-iron skiff, and meant to be built the same way, by pulling preshaped sides around some frames and screwing the bottom on. No proper lofting or rigid building jig are needed. I don't see how a real sailboat, with as good a performance and as few vices as most, could be put together, one-off, much quicker than this one, or out of cheaper materials.

She is stiff for her weight, roomy, and comfortable to sit in as long as the strength of the wind and the sail you carry allows staying down on the bottom; the gunwale is a bit thin for comfortable hiking-out. Use of the clip-on leeboard makes more room available, and the rig was picked because the high partner thwart can be eliminated for sprawling space. The balanced club jib is the only self-tending type that needs no sheet horse across the boat to set well; the upward pull on the luff does the job of holding the

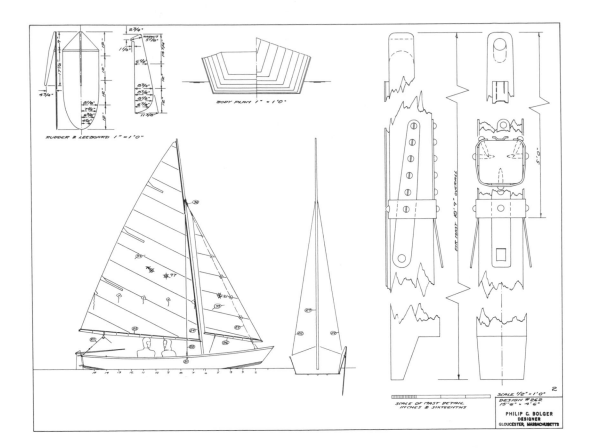

clew down. The whole rig is also so easy to dismantle that there's no temptation to leave the mast standing on a mooring, or when rowing. As for the last, she's too wide on the bottom to be a really good rowboat, but as an auxiliary she's not to be sneered at and a good man could certainly get over a mile in twenty minutes in her in a dead calm. The oars are a clutter in the boat, but they are nowhere near the nuisance that an outboard motor would be, and are a lot cheaper and prettier besides. Oars are actually not so terribly in the way in a sailboat when stowed down the centerline under your knees; they could also be fitted with racks to stow above the gunwale and sticking out over the stern, or they could even be stood up against the mast or shrouds.

This boat will only weigh 130 pounds or so stripped, will come smoothly up onto the lightest kind of trailer, and can be angled into a garage corner and still leave space for a small car. To my eye she is a clean and graceful boat that doesn't look cheap, and her layout and behavior may be better for, say, a young family, than a shorter dinghy of the same weight and cost, or a racing machine designed to give two strong boys a strenuous day. Perhaps she may be forgiven for not being a dory.

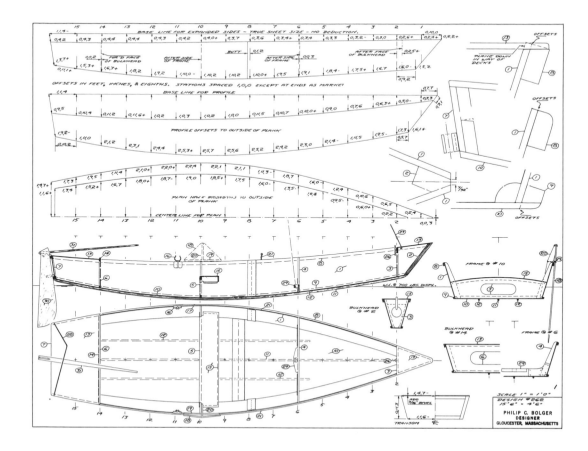

KEY TO PLANS

Many more dimensions are given than are needed for the assembly method specified; this is to allow the designed shape to be adapted to other methods of construction, also to allow a check on the general accuracy of the drawings.

Plywood: all ¼″ fir, marine or exterior grade in 4′ x 8′ sheets; exterior grade will probably have more and larger voids in the internal courses than marine; these ought to be plugged up as far as possible when found.

Natural wood for stringers, fastening frames, etc., to be Douglas fir, mahogany, white pine, cedar, or spruce, or any wood having good gluing properties; avoid oak, teak, yellow pine.

All joints glued with resorcinol or epoxy glue; length of fastenings is noted; these can be bronze or Everdur screws, or Monel Anchorfast nails; at plank butts rivets, clinch nails, or bolts may be used.

1. Hull sides plywood, made up to diagrammed pattern; ¼″ x 4″ butt straps; note that the stations used for dimensioning on this diagram are not the same as the same-numbered stations on the lines proper, the difference being 2⅝″ in the case of the #2 bulkhead. Mark for the frames and bulkheads on the pattern and on the sides themselves.

Richard Ramsey's Featherwind
on an Indiana lake

2. Stem from ¾″ x 1½″ secured to one of the sides and bevelled at the given angle to take the other side.

3. Forward (#2) bulkhead plywood, with ½″ x 2½″ fastening frame and ¾″ square pieces at the sides; bevel at sides ¼″.

4. Frame at #6: bottom piece ¾″ x 3½″, side frames from ¾″ x 2½″; gussets plywood; ¾″ screws or nails. Bevel of sides 3/16″, on bottom 3/32″.

5. Midships frame (#10): plywood web with 5″ x 17″ hole (for oar stowage); top of web crowned about 2½″; fastening frames ¾″ x 1½″ top and bottom; side frames from ¾″ x 2½″ tapered to 1½″ near gunwale; no bevel.

6. After bulkhead (#14): plywood with 6″ x 18″ hole (for stowage); fastening frames ½″ x ¾″ and ½″ x 1½″; bevel ⅛″ sides and bottom.

(Make these four frames and bulkheads from offsets given for their numbered stations, deducting ¼″ for planking.)

7. Transom plywood: ½″ x 1½″ fastening frame; for those wishing to skip complete lofting, dimensions are given for the transom at the inside of the frame; note that these, and all the bevels given, are only correct if the designed total thickness is retained. Transom bevel 5/32″ sides, 9/32″ bottom, 3/16″ (the other way) top or deck.

(Secure the sides together at the stem, standing them on edge for the purpose; spring them back around the bulkheads and frames, each lined up on its marks, and secure to them and to the transom with glue and ¾″ screws or nails.)

8. Gunwale stringers ¾″ x 1½″, clamped, with glue, to outside of sides, and ¾″ screws or nail driven from inside.

9. Chine logs ¾″ square, on outside of sides, secured as with gunwale stringers; bevel to take bottom.

10. Bottom plywood; ¼″ x 6″ butt strap; ¾″ screws or nails to chine logs, frames, etc.

11. Shoe ¾″ x 1″ sprung on to outside of bottom after hull is assembled; glue on; ¾″ screws from inside.

12. Side bottom guard stringers ¾″ square about 9′ long.

13. Decking at bow and stern plywood; sheets of dense foam up to 4″ thick may be inserted under decks for extra buoyancy and stability when swamped.

14. Coaming ¾″ square.

15. Thwart ¼″ plywood sprung to about 2½″ crown, glued and screwed down on web frame; ¾″ square fastening strip each side; ½″ x 2½″ stiffener with top edge sawn to crown, along forward edge. Note slot each side for leeboard hook.

16. Davis-type oarlocks: pair eight-foot ash oars not shown.

17. Plane gunwale stringer flat for leeboard to bear.

18. Leeboard (only one needed, but one on each side if builder is troubled by asymmetry) double ¼″ or single ½″ plywood with edges well sharpened; 1′ 6″ maximum breadth, 4′ 0″ long overall.

19. Leeboard crosspiece ¾″ square by 1′ 6″.

20. Leeboard hook from ¾″ x 2½″; two ¼″ bolts through leeboard; hook fits over gunwale as shown, through slot in thwart #15; hole through web #5 and hook for a pin to keep the leeboard from floating up when the boat heels; crosspiece serves as vertical stop; thwart and frame hold it fore-and-aft.

21. Shroud lanyard ½″ dacron through hole in gunwale stringer with stopper knot underneath; eye splice around thimble for snap hook of shroud.

22. Shrouds ⅛″ stainless wire about 12′ long each; swaged jaw fittings on upper ends, snap hooks on lower; adjust roughly by stopper knot position, set up tight with jib halyard.

23. Forward preventer ¼″ dacron spliced into becket of jib block, led down through cringles on axis of jib, to stopper knot under hole in foredeck.

24. Mast solid fir or spruce, oblong section 2″ x 2″ lower half, tapered to 1¾″ x 1¾″ at shroud attachments, to 1″ x 1″ at truck; 18′ 9″ overall; see full-size detail for shape at heel and truck hole; tang assembled from 1/16″ x ¾″ x 6″ stainless steel or brass with ¾″ round-head screws to mast; ⅝″ track and slides.

25. Main boom ¾″ plank, 9′ 10″ long, 2½″ deep at sheet block 2′ 0″ from clew end, tapered to 1½″ each end; ¼″ plywood jaw set into mast end.

26. Jib club ¾″ x 4′ 9″ plank, 2½″ at pennant attachment 10″ in from for'd end, tapered to 1″ each end. Pennant ⅜″ dacron spliced around club and tail belayed to 5″ wood cleat bolted (not screwed) to #2 bulkhead; sheet single part led to pin in #6 frame.

27. Main sheet ¼″ nylon; snap hook to traveller horse; a light plastic block on a sling around the boom.

28. Sheet traveller horse ⅜″ nylon; stopper knot under gunwale stringer each side.

29. Mast step retaining block from 1½″ x 2″ x 12″ secured to frame with two ¼″ bolts and some screws.

30. Rudder blade double ¼″ or single ½″ plywood; standard pintles and gudgeons any make.

31. Tiller from ¾″ x 2″ x 4′ 0″; ¼″ bolt to blade; tiller stows along back of rudder blade.

32. Jib halyard ⅜″ dacron led over a light shackle becket block like Race-

Lite #RL-304-B and down to cleat near foot of mast.

33.   Jib 11' 6" luff, 9' 6" leach, 4' 7" foot; note cringles for preventer; luff of jib should be roped or in some way well reinforced.

34.   Mainsail 16' 0" luff, 16' 10" leach (clew to shoulder of headboard), 9' 8" foot; roach and battens to sailmaker's judgment; one row or reef points; lash to boom with separate ties, not lacing.

16

NINA

16'0" x 4'0"

Henry Gibson explained that he wanted a larger sport fishing boat than the one he'd been using; he fished, he said, in the Gulf Stream off Palm Beach and over towards Bimini. I was just going to ask if he had diesel or gasoline power in mind when he explained that he always went alone and preferred to launch his boat off the open beach near his home rather than come around from Lake Worth, whereupon he showed me a picture of the Sunfish sailboard he'd been using, with a sailfish about half the size of the boat lashed on its deck. One of the advantages of this kind of fishing, he said, was that the fish you caught looked much bigger and more impressive than they would lying in a far corner of a Rybovich cockpit; this was manifestly true from the photo. He showed diagrams of how his rods were supported, and of the frameless kites he used instead of outriggers to trail his bait. He hoped the new, custom-built boat would be somewhat better in surf than the Sunfish, but what he mainly wanted was something in which his toes would be less exposed to shark-bite when he spilled blood from a caught fish.

The strange but rather attractive deck shape that eventually emerged was mostly the owner's work. He had all sorts of things that had to be lashed down on it, and some that it was desirable to be able to drop momentarily without necessarily losing them overboard; since he was often out many hours there ought to be a wide choice of positions and postures, so as not to get too stiff and cramped. As for the proportions and hull form, you have to bear in mind that the safety requirements of a sailboard are just about the opposite of most types of sailboats: there is no danger in capsizing, which you can do (and I've done myself) a dozen times a day or whenever you feel like a swim, but there is some point in worrying about falling off it without a capsize so that the boat sails away without you. When I'm sailing one of these things I make a point of keeping two or three turns of the sheet around my wrist, to be sure of pulling the boat over if I should

Henry Gibson trolling from Niña *off Palm Beach*

fall off it. The boat should have a very short range of stability, just the sort that is dangerous in any other type of boat, stiff when loaded and up-right but quick to turn over on her side at any sudden excuse. The combination of considerable deadrise, a hard chine, and a fairly tall rig was supposed to work in this direction; she is probably a little too wide to be a sure thing not to sail away from you, but it's not likely that she would get far in the open sea on her own without falling over.

The owner was not much interested in speed. He wanted a docile, weatherly, all-around boat with special emphasis on going through surf. He questioned me sharply several times during the designing about her qualities as a surfboat, and now praises them as they've worked out in practice. I gave her rather more powerful lines forward than seems to be best for outright speed, and a correspondingly narrower stern; I'm inclined to think I overdid it on both counts but he doesn't agree. The pivoted centerboard and rudder were of course included so you could sail straight in on the beach without having to pull them up at just the right moment. The triangular board also is less sensitive than a deeper and narrower daggerboard when the boat is being sailed with something less than perfect attention, as when distracted by a big fish.

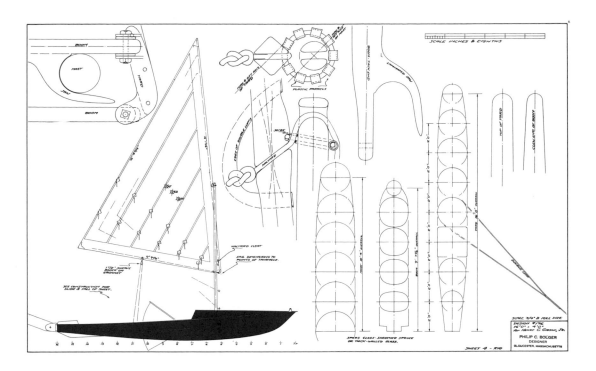

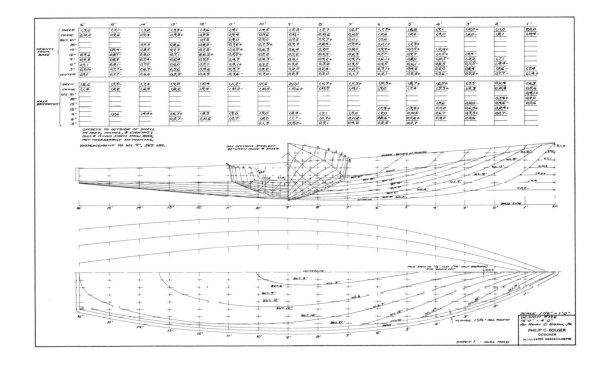

She was built without a skeg because I thought she would be easier to drag on the beach, but it appeared at once that she would have to have one if the tiller was to be left free for an instant. The one shown tamed her somewhat but it should have been bigger and deeper; I think it would have been better to give her a short, deep one in line with the transom and use it to support the leading edge of the rudder; it could be eight or ten inches deep, all abaft station #15, and would steady the boat better and also improve the effectiveness of the rudder, maybe even to the point where the deep swinging blade could be eliminated.

The boom lateen rig works well, including the reefing arrangement, though as the height doesn't come down much when reefed the main advantage is that she can heel much more without tripping on her boom when reefed. She has spars made from glass vaulting poles instead of the sheathed wooden one shown, so I have no test of the proportions indicated; as rigged the mast and yard bend more than they should, and the boom not as much as it should. From their proportions I infer that the designed spars might work pretty well.

I'm no enthusiast for fiberglass one-off construction, and would much rather have had her molded plywood or even strip-built. But I must say that Brandt Custom Boat in Palm Beach made a high class job of her, flawless, in fact, as far as I can see, and she has apparently stood up well for some years of fairly rough treatment. The sequence was: .015 gel coat; .012

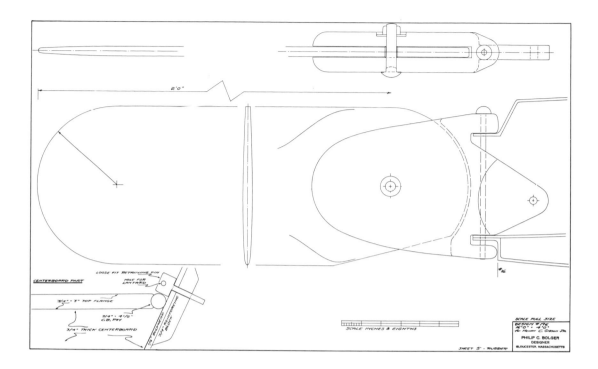

55 percent HDK fiber and resin; six layers 7.5 ounce cloth, single layup, approximately 45 percent glass; abaft bulkhead added one layer 24 ounce woven roving. Deck the same. She weighed about 160 pounds, stripped, which is more than a wooden boat of reasonable rigidity should, in spite of the foam bulkheads which I copied from a British dinghy design, by David Thomas as I remember it.

I admire the principle behind this boat very much. I'm no enemy of motorboats, but it distresses me that so many people don't know or think that you can go anywhere or do anything without machinery, or rather, since this boat is in fact a very efficient machine, without internal-combustion machinery. Henry Gibson very plausibly argues that he goes as far in this boat as he would in a conventional fishing cruiser, with much less wasted motion getting started and at least equal safety when you come to add up what can happen. Niña was naturally fabulously expensive; I suppose you could buy ten production sailboards for what was in her by the time she sailed, but even so all that money wouldn't have bought one of the engines for the kind of boat most people think you should have to fish the Gulf Stream, or paid one year's depreciation on such a boat. And all logic and rationalizing aside, have you ever in your life seen a more superb example of cheerful, competent, one-up-manship?

17

MOUSER

16′0″ x 6′6″ x 1′3″

This cat was built in Mississippi as a trailer boat. Last time I heard of her she was fifteen years old, seemingly in good shape including her original sail, and said by her owner at that time to be faster than most boats he crossed tacks with. Nobody I know of has accused her of being a pretty boat, but she is apparently a rather good one.

The design was supposed to be an improvement on a Chesapeake-designed cat built by my elder brother and given to me when I was thirteen or fourteen, about this length and weight and with a similar sail plan, but narrower and lower and afflicted with an exciting tendency to go end over end when driven hard off the wind. The high and full chine line shown here appears to have dealt with that failing and probably helps her on the wind as well by giving her added buoyancy to lean on when she starts to heel.

It looks to me now as though I was too full of the "long, clean run" talk that was in vogue at the time the design was made. She has her center of buoyancy very far forward by my present habits of design, and I don't think that is particularly good either for windward ability or for all-round handling qualities. However, the doctrine of the long run was not by any means all foolishness and very likely this boat is faster under the right conditions of loading, wind, and water than she would be the way I would do it now; she obviously does have the makings of a great burst of speed now and then when reaching in smooth water.

The peculiar centerboard was due to the original owner's wish to be able to lift it out easily for travelling. I forget now why that seemed important but it's always a convenience. I was afraid it was too small and that the open-topped case was dangerously low to the waterline, but it's apparently all right on both counts.

The construction is not very imaginative but as put together by Mr. E. H. Arthur of Gulfport it seems to have stood up well. It's the sort of thing that used to be touted as easy for amateurs because it didn't have steam-bent

Mouser *at age 15*

frames; I doubt that whoever first produced this idea had thought through
the tricky bevelling involved, or of how to get neatly through the transition
from lap to butt along the chine up forward. Nowadays I'd be inclined to
use plywood above the chine, as it would save some seams, increase the
rigidity, and eliminate the intermediate frames there; 3/8" plywood would
be thick enough. The massive keel was in imitation of the Chesapeake
cat's best feature; it gives a solid base for trailering (though I certainly
ought to have given it a little bit of projecting shoe to keep the flanges of
the trailer rollers away from the garboards), is not to be sneered at as
ballast, and always gave me the feeling that in combination with the plumb
stem it would prove an effective ram if somebody forced my right of way.
This last idea I never got a good chance to test. Made of oak or hard pine
as specified, this keel is a great test of the builder's ability at sharpening
tools.

The rig was copied straight from the older cat. For low-cost power it's
not easy to see how to improve it much. It's especially good when reefed,
as you're left with effective area on a comically low height and very little
windage of any sort. Before the wind, every inch of it (and there are a lot
of inches for her size) is pulling. I won a lot of handicap races in my old
boat by her speed off the wind combined with her deceptively stodgy appearance when pointed out to the handicapping committee. There's a lot
more satisfaction in a boat which is faster than she looks than in the con-
verse situation.

KEY TO PLAN

1. Keel sided $4\frac{1}{2}''$ oak or equal; $\frac{1}{4}''$ bolts to floor timbers, stem knee, and skeg.

2. Stem and knee sided $3''$ oak or equal; stem extends above deck about $3''$ with $\frac{3}{8}''$ x $5\frac{1}{2}''$ brass pin to form mooring bitt.

3. Skeg sided $2''$ oak or equal planed off to $1\frac{1}{4}''$ at trailing edge; $\frac{1}{4}''$ rods about as shown.

4. Centerboard case $1''$ oak or equal with $\frac{1}{4}''$ drifts from keel, and rods as in centerboard.

5. Headblocks $1\frac{1}{2}''$ x $3''$ oak or equal.

6. Centerboard $1''$ thick oak or equal, with $\frac{1}{4}''$ rods, lead insert as shown, $\frac{1}{2}''$ manila pennant, pin hole for raised position; pivot pin is $1''$ pipe threaded through board, working in U-shaped, brass-shod slot in top of case for ready removal. Board and case must be well-seasoned stock or warpage may be troublesome; plywood is not reliable.

7. $\frac{3}{8}''$ brass belaying pins for centerboard pennant and mainsheet.

8. Thwart $1''$ x $3''$ oak or equal flush with coaming each side, bent up over centerboard case to $1''$ crown; $2''$ screws to coaming and sides of centerboard case.

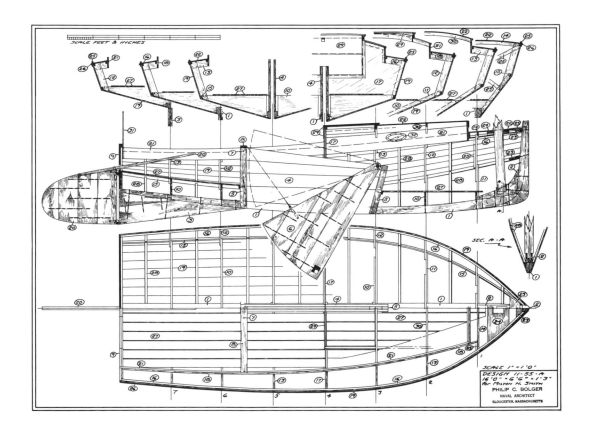

9. Transom ¾″ plywood; ¾″ oak or equal backing.

10. Floor timbers ¾″ oak or hard pine.

11. Bottom frames (station #1, 2, & 3 only) ¾″ x 1½″ oak or equal.

12. Topside frames ¾″ x 1½″ oak or equal.

13. Short beams ¾″ x 3″ with straight top edge.

14. One full deck beam ¾″ x 1½″, crown as given.

15. Chines ¾″ x 1½″ oak or equal, bevelled about as shown.

16. Clamps ¾″ x 1″ oak or equal.

17. Bulkhead ½″ fir plywood; ¾″ fastening frame about as shown.

18. Deck header ¾″ x 1″ oak or equal.

19. Bottom and topside planking ½″ cedar or equal.

20. Rudder 1¼″ oak or equal, ¼″ rods; tiller mahogany sided 1¼″, 4′ 8″ overall, removable from under straps.

21. Coaming and trunk side ⅝″ mahogany or equal; full-glued and 1½″ screws to deck header all around.

22. Deck and trunk top ⅜″ fir plywood; may be covered with canvas or plastic; ⅝″ x 6″ butt blocks as convenient.

23. Breasthooks at chine and clamp 1″ oak or equal, with ¼″ bolts through stem; upper breast shaped to crown of deck; deck and clamps must be very strongly secured to it.

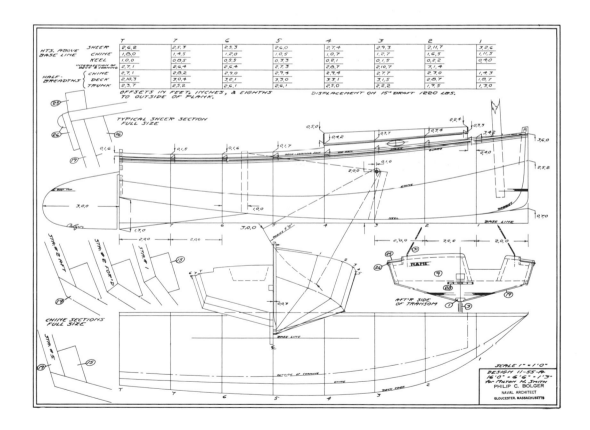

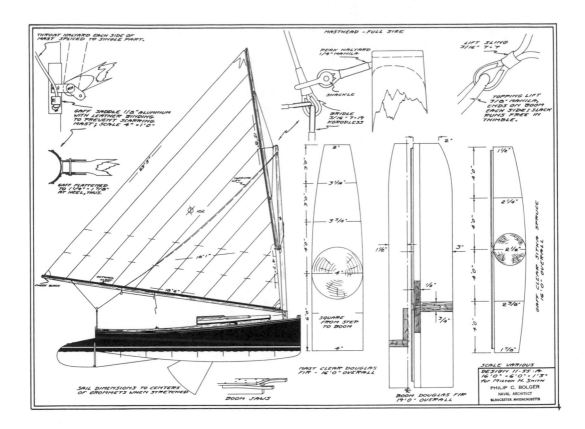

24. Partner beam 1″ x 10″ oak or equal; steam to slight curve and trim up to fit snugly under deck; glue and screw strongly to deck all across.

25. Diagonal struts ¾″ x 1½″ oak or equal, bolted together where they cross; also ¾″ square toe rail of mahogany all around deck.

26. Sheer molding ¼″ x 1½″ with ½″ half-round, mahogany.

27. Floorboards ½″ x 4″ cedar or equal; fasten to floor timbers with screws for ready removal; sections for'd and aft of centerboard case laid loose for pumping.

28. Planking cleats ¾″ x 1″ oak or equal; fasten to planking only.

29. Companion slides ⅜″ fir plywood; sliding hatch opens 24″ x 36″.

30. Trunk beams ¾″ x 1½″ oak or equal.

31. Traveler horse ⅜″ round bar about as shown to clear outboard motor.

32. Deadlight port and starboard ⅛″ clear plastic with ⅝″ round head screws to trunk side.

33. Outboard motor 5 to 10 OBC h.p.; six knots will be about limit of speed.

18
LYNX

14'8" x 6'11" x 3'0"

Lynx was built under the eye of publicity, an enterprising local reporter having been taken with the comedy of this minuscule boat occupying the ways of the ancient Story Shipyard at Essex, builders of the giant racing fishing schooners. "Enchanting" and "adorable" were words heard at the launching party, but there was some skepticism about the behavior of a boat on such extreme proportions.

The first doubt resolved was the workability of the cabin and cockpit layout, both of which turned out almost unbelievably roomy and free of inconveniences. Trials dispelled qualms about her ability: she proved close-winded, went where she looked, balanced well heeled as well as upright, maneuvered neatly, and (what I had worried about) shouldered her way through a turmoil of motorboat wakes in light airs without pitching twice in the same hole. She's remarkably dry in a chop, and will hold her course with tiller lashed on a wide range of points. She doesn't seem to care where people sit fore-and-aft; if they sit to leeward she heels sharply in a breeze but keeps right on sailing. It seems absurd to describe a boat on such proportions as fast, and the light racing centerboarders of her length certainly can sail by her without much trouble, but she keeps snapping at their heels even dead to windward and gets over an amazing amount of sea. In fact she has exceeded expectations in every respect, including, I must say, in what she cost, close to a thousand hours of labor having gone into her first and last.

She began with an announcement for a design competition for a "pocket cruiser." Thus stimulated, I doodled a number of studies of what the smallest, or rather shortest, possible boat might be that would be fit to keep the sea without worrying too much about the weather, be comfortable indefinitely for a singlehander, and provide sprawling space for a congenial couple for a weekend or for a young family day-sailing. One sketch stood out from the others and caught the eye of John Williamson when he

Lynx *with the author at the tiller*

dropped in to see me. That was in the fall of 1971. John was just out of the hospital after an unsuccessful cancer operation. The disease had cut into his strength and forced him to dispose of his heavy auxiliary; he'd been told he would die in the spring, to which his reaction was, roughly, "If I do that I'll miss the summer sailing. I'll die in the fall, *if then.*" A man with no lack of nerve, who regards death as an enemy, can make a good fight of it with that attitude, a fight that John has had the better of so far.* He ordered the boat from Story for an amusement during the long winter and as suitable for his diminished strength for the summer sailing. She is a type that can take care of her crew, rather than continually drawing on them for her own safety. She's a well-corked bottle and it's not easy to imagine conditions that would put her down. Compared with *Sopranino,* to say nothing about *Tinkerbell,* she's a powerful roomy vessel able enough to go anywhere.

A criticism of the design that I regard with respect is the comment that she's a caricature of the results of the fallacy that "short is small." Her midsection is that of quite a normal twenty-footer and she's not so very much cheaper to build than the twenty would be. But she is some cheaper. The comparison with the *Quickstep* design is somewhat interesting. *Quickstep* is five feet longer, a foot narrower, a foot shallower, and about the same sail area, displacement, and, presumably, cost. It can hardly be doubted that she would sail six miles to *Lynx's* five under most conditions, but it's equally definite that her cabin and cockpit are both much less roomy and all-around less comfortable. In this size range, the extra hull freeboard of *Lynx* makes an important difference; though she was expensive for her

*John Williamson died February 13, 1973, age 45.

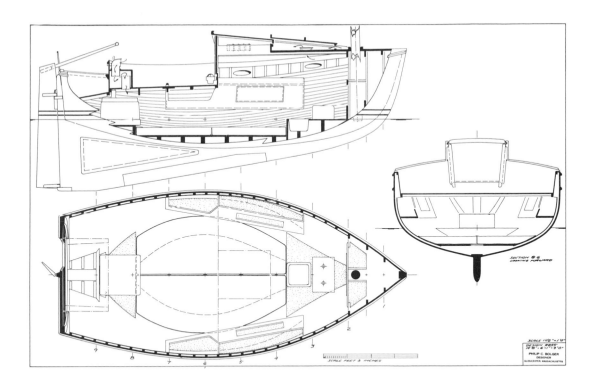

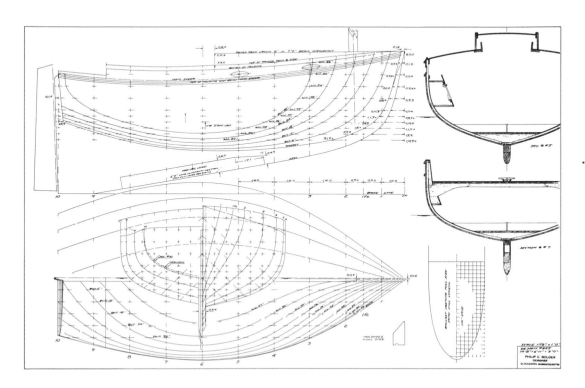

length, she is not so for her amenities. An additional outlay would add space out of proportion to the amount, but it's not so easy to see how you could get as much for the same outlay by juggling the proportions differently.

Lynx's qualities have led one or two people to speculate about scaling her up to a larger size. If you just built her with the bow further from the stern on the same sections, you'd have a normal sort of boat but the keel would have to be altered in some way; she has a long keel as built in the sense that it runs the full length of the boat and then some, but it's not long in proportion to her rig and displacement and I doubt would work so nicely if you stretched it out the full length of a longer boat. However, I was going to say that if you doubled her size all over you would have a very, very roomy thirty-footer, and I think an able and fast one—with a thirty-five-foot main boom and 750-square-foot mainsail. If there is one main reason for the surprisingly good performance of the boat, it's the size, and height, of her sail plan and that rig scaled proportionately for a bigger boat would quickly begin to look frightening to a modern eye, though a hundred years ago nobody would have thought much about it. As a matter of fact, with suitable gear and in a boat that can be counted on to recover from any kind of a knockdown, a big, long-boomed mainsail isn't in the same class as a man-eater with some of the popular headsails nowadays.

The bent-frame carvel construction was used for *Lynx* partly because it's well established as long-lived, but mostly because this type of framing lends itself to an inner sheathing protecting the interior of the cabin from bilge-water and condensation, and promotes transverse air circulation through the frame bays, which tends to keep her cool in summer, warm in cold weather, and dry at all times; in short it makes a more comfortable cabin than any of the constructions in which you live in contact with the outer skin no matter how finished off. The other obvious possibility would be strip-planking, glued or not; it could be very thick, all of an inch, and still probably come out quite a bit lighter than the carvel, and there would be a noticeable gain in space inside, at the price of damp mattresses now and then. There is no reason not to consider the other usual constructions, bearing in mind that any great saving in weight will just mean you'll have to add more ballast or else put up with a corky, tiddly action when somebody moves around on deck.

The plans are shown as handed to the builder. Various small changes were made such as the oblong ports in place of the elliptical ones designed, and others, similarly matters of taste. The sailmaker and owner ganged up on me to have the cat on the sail jumping the wrong direction as I see it. The one-legged companionway step is on a separate drawing because I didn't figure out how it ought to go until the boat was far along in construction. Apart from this last, I see absolutely nothing that I myself am anxious to change, though if I happened to be trying to keep the cost down I would think about leaving off the jib temporarily or permanently; she sails very well without it and it spends a great deal of its time rolled up to save handling its sheets.

KEY TO CONSTRUCTION PLAN

1. Stem, knee, and keel sided $3\frac{1}{2}$" mahogany or oak; knee bolts $\frac{3}{8}$" bronze.
2. Shoe forward and abaft ballast sided $3\frac{1}{2}$" mahogany or oak; $\frac{1}{4}$" bronze bolts and lags.
3. Skeg sided $3\frac{1}{2}$" mahogany or oak.
4. Sternpost sided $2\frac{1}{2}$" mahogany or oak, $1\frac{1}{2}$" on trailing edge and hollowed slightly to clear around leading edge of rudder blade; halved and bolted to keel; four $\frac{3}{8}$" bronze bolts through transom; $\frac{1}{4}$" drifts to skeg and filler block.
5. Filler block sided $3\frac{1}{2}$" softwood.
6. Cover sheets of deadwood $\frac{1}{2}$" fir plywood rabbetted into keel, skeg, and filler block; about $1\frac{1}{4}$" bronze screws spaced 3" at most all around with heads exposed — no glue.
7. Ballast casting lead, same section full length except for forward top corner knocked off as dimensioned; total weight about 500 pounds; seven $\frac{1}{2}$" bronze bolts through keel and floor timbers; half-oval bronze or stainless steel rub molding on bottom of keel extends from bow to stern.

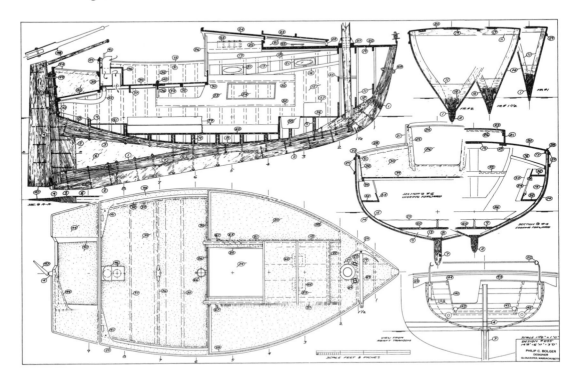

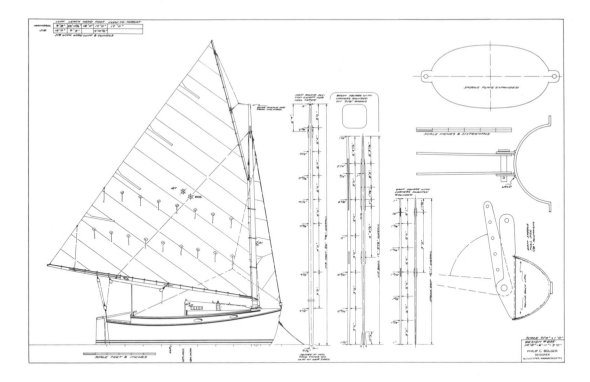

8.   Apron ¾″ x 5½″ oak or mahogany; 1½″ screws to keel and skeg.

9.   Floor timbers oak or mahogany; six under sole flat sided 2″; others 1½″.

10.   Transom 1¼″ mahogany, edge-nailed; fashion pieces at sides about ⅞″; no frame along the bottom.

11.   Three sawn frames at the bow from ⅞″ mahogany or fir, molded about as shown; ¼″ bolts.

12.   Cheeks of mast step 1½″ x 2½″ oak or mahogany; six ¼″ bolts through knee; drill to drain step effectively.

13.   Bent frames about ⅞″ x 1¼″ oak on 6″ centers.

14.   Planking about ⅝″ mahogany; 1¼″ Everdur or bronze screws; fifteen or sixteen strakes to a side.

15.   Ceiling ¼″ soft pine or cedar; laid tight from #2 frame to the last bent frame at the stern.

16.   Ceiling clamp ¾″ x 1½″ mahogany.

17.   Deck clamp ¾″ by about 2½″ mahogany; saw and bevel top edge to meet deck without forcing.

18.   Deck stringers ¾″ x 3½″ mahogany or fir.

19.   Deck centerline butt strap ½″ x 8″ plywood.

20.   Raised deck ½″ fir plywood, sheathed with glass cloth and polyester resin; butt sheets along centerline; about 1¼″ screws or barbed nails to edge of sheer strake, deck clamp, etc. Deck crown does not vary if the designed "powderhorn" sheer is maintained; a temporary beam about station #4 will be needed until the companionway shroud is in place to hold the shape.

	10	9	8	7	6	5	4	3	2	1½	1
HEIGHTS FROM BASE LINE											
RAISED DECK			5.4.1+	5.3.6+	5.4.2+	5.5.0+	5.6.2	5.8.0	5.9.7+	5.10.6+	5.11.3+
MOLDING			5.2.1	5.1.6+	5.2.1	5.3.0	5.4.2	5.6.0	5.8.2	5.9.4+	5.10.6+
MAIN SHEER	5.0.5	4.10.4	4.9.2	4.8.7	4.9.2+	4.10.4	5.0.2	5.2.5+	5.5.5+	5.7.3+	5.9.2
BUT. 30"		3.5.5+	2.11.1+	2.7.3+	2.6.3	2.8.2	3.2.1+	4.10.3			
24"	3.8.7	3.1.4	2.8.2	2.4.5+	2.3.4	2.5.0	2.9.4+	3.8.0			
18"	3.5.1	2.11.2	2.6.2	2.2.5+	2.1.4	2.2.4+	2.6.2	3.1.6	4.7.5+		
12"	3.3.0	2.9.4+	2.4.4	2.1.0+	1.11.6+	2.0.5+	2.3.3	2.8.6+	3.8.6	4.9.5	
6"	3.1.4+	2.8.0	2.3.0	1.11.6	1.10.4	1.10.7	2.0.5+	2.4.2	2.11.4	3.7.0	4.10.5
RABBET	3.0.6	2.6.7+	2.2.0+	1.10.7+	1.7.4+	1.9.5+	1.10.7	2.1.0+	2.5.0+	2.8.7	3.5.0
KEEL	0.0.0	0.0.0	0.3.1	0.6.2	0.9.3+	1.0.4	1.3.5	1.7.1	2.9.0	2.3.7	2.0.3
HALF-BREADTHS											
DECK	2.5.0	2.9.6+	3.1.6+	3.4.4+	3.5.5	3.4.5	3.1.0+	2.6.5	1.9.1	1.3.4	0.9.2+
W.L. 66"			3.15+					2.6.5	1.8.6+	1.2.5	0.7.7
60"	2.5.0		3.1.6+	3.4.4+	3.5.5	3.4.5	3.1.0	2.6.2	1.7.4+	1.0.7	0.6.3
54"	2.9.6	2.9.6+	3.1.6+	3.4.4+	3.5.5	3.4.4	3.0.6	2.5.1	1.5.2	0.10.5	0.9.7
48"	2.2.6	2.9.2	3.1.5	3.4.3	3.5.3+	3.4.0	2.11.6	2.2.6	1.2.0	0.8.1	0.3.3
42"	1.7.7	2.6.2	3.0.2	3.3.4	3.4.2	3.2.4	2.9.1	1.10.2+	0.10.2	0.5.4+	0.2.0
39"	1.0.0	2.2.5+	2.10.3	3.2.2	3.3.0	3.1.0	2.6.6+	1.7.3+	0.8.2+	0.4.3	0.1.2+
36"	0.0.7	1.8.1	2.7.2	3.0.0	3.1.1	2.10.5	2.3.4+	1.4.0	0.6.3	0.3.1	0.0.5+
33"	0.0.6+	0.9.7	2.1.6	2.8.4+	2.10.0	2.7.1	1.11.0	1.0.2	0.4.3	0.1.6+	
30"	0.0.6	0.1.6	1.5.2+	2.3.1	2.5.3	2.2.1+	1.5.4+	0.8.2	0.2.3	0.9.7+	
27"	0.9.6	0.1.6	0.6.0	1.7.0	1.10.5	1.7.0+	0.11.1+	0.4.2+	0.1.5		

OFFSETS IN FEET, INCHES, & EIGHTHS
TO OUTSIDE OF PLANK. PLUS MARKS (+)
INDICATE BIAS, NOT SIXTEENTHS.

DESIGN #255
14'8" x 6'11" x 3'0"

21. Companionway sides ¾" mahogany, with grooves for slide added by gluing on battens; screw deck into sides from below with 1½" (or longer) screws spaced about 3".

22. For'd end of companion shroud about ⅞" mahogany with two vent slots each about 1½" x 10".

23. Companion shroud ½" plywood; same crown as deck; two ¾" x 1½" sawn beams on top.

24. Companion hatch ½" plywood; same crown as deck; slides in grooves in shroud sides.

25. Companion hatch coaming ¾" x 3½" mahogany.

26. Companion slide ½" plywood; no openings or stiffeners.

27. Mast partner coaming about 1¼" high mahogany or fir grooved on the outside for lashing of mast coat.

28. Toe rail about ¾" square mahogany.

29. Moldings ¾" x 1½" mahogany; see full-size section.

30. Raised deck bulkhead ½" plywood.

31. Cockpit clamp ¾" x 1" fir.

32. Cockpit sheathing ¼" plywood, blocked off bent frames with shims as shown.

33. Cockpit rail cap ½" plywood.

34. Cockpit sole stringer ¾" x 1½" fir.

35. Forward cockpit beam 1½" square oak or mahogany.

36. Center beam (under ½" x 6" athwartships plywood butt strap) sided ¾", about 6½" at sides with ½" plywood knees as shown; 1¾" molded over berth cushions.

37. Beam ¾" x 3½" oak or mahogany.

38. Bulkhead ½" plywood, forms after end of cockpit and forward end of motor well.

39. Cockpit sole flat ½" plywood, fiberglass-sheathed.

40. Sides and bottom of motor and fuel well ½" plywood.

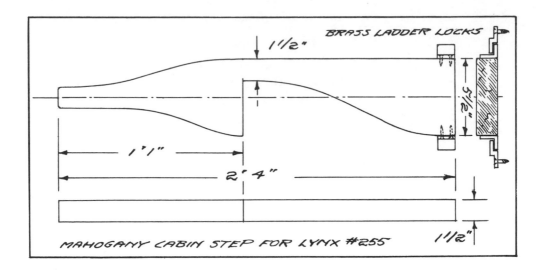

MAHOGANY CABIN STEP FOR LYNX #255

41.   Knee, forming continuation of rail cap with ¾" mahogany backing; slot for ¾" x 3" x 3' 6" boom crutch each side (only one crutch, to be placed one side or the other); removable ½" x 8" belaying pin each side for jib sheets and stern warps.

42.   Cockpit scuppers 1¼" diameter; neoprene hoses to transom outlets.

43.   Motor well scuppers.

44.   Afterdeck ½" plywood, crowned about 1" at transom.

45.   Main sheet cleat 8" wood or hollow bronze, bolted through sole.

46.   Watertrap vent with 4" diameter pipes; low cowl of flexible plastic like Manhatten #G-421.

47.   Rudder blade sided 1½" oak, tapered to ½" trailing edge; five galvanized ¼" drift rods; special cast bronze gudgeons, pintle, and heel fitting.

48.   Tiller from 1½" x 3" x 3' 6" mahogany; ¼" bronze end plates and ½" pin.

49.   Loose pin to stop rudder from floating off.

50.   Traveller horse ½" bronze rod bolted to outside of transom; rope or wood traveller stops.

51.   Clear plastic deadlights screwed to inside of planking.

52.   Shelves.

53.   Shelf and locker facing forms backrest.

54.   Panel removable.

55.   Shelf each side of mast.

56.   Dresser flat ½" plywood, Formica-sheathed.

57.   Alcohol stove; if two-burner as shown, cut off back lower corners to fit.

58.   Removable plastic sink; no drain.

59.   Foam mattresses, 4" thick; each in two sections connected at the top as shown, to fold away under the cockpit.

60.   Cabin sole ¾" teak or iroko; center plank about 6" wide left loose and in two sections butted on floor timber abaft station #5, to lift out for bailing;

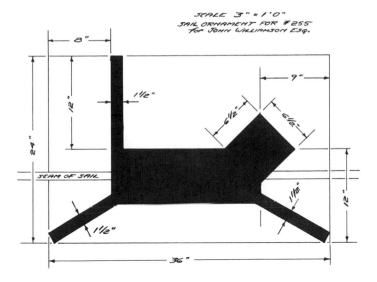

otherwise make sole and ceiling as tight as possible to keep bilgewater away from the bedding.

61. Platform for Thetford Porta Potti or other chemical toilet; if necessary, cut away ceiling to take after corners of toilet.

62. Holes in deck, about 4″ square, with flanged coamings about 1¼″ above deck (outlet vents for stove and lamp heat).

63. Louvered holes in companion shroud sides, opening aft.

64. Double deck halyard block, for main peak and throat halyards.

65. Single deck halyard block for jib halyard.

66. Spherical compass removable from bracket.

67. Two five-inch cleats for main halyards starboard side; one six-inch cleat for jib halyard port side.

68. Bronze shoulder eye bolt, ½″ x 6″, for mooring pennant.

69. Yachtsman 15-pound anchor with stock wired in place; a Herreshoff-type three-piece 25-pound anchor can be lashed up under one of the lower cabin shelves along with a six-foot boathook.

Rigging list (all dacron except topping lifts)

Main peak halyard ⅜″: from span on gaff, through hole in masthead, down through deck block, aft to cleat on companionway shroud.

Main throat halyard ⅜″: from gaff saddle, through side shackle block on mast sling, down through deck block, aft to cleat.

Jib halyard ½″: from swivel on head of jib luff wire, through side-shackle block on mast sling, down through deck block, aft to cleat on companionway shroud.

Gaff span ⅜″: spliced around gaff each end.

Topping lifts ½″ nylon: spliced around mast, down through boom cheeks, set up with stopper knots under cheeks to support boom three or four inches clear of the main hatch when the lifts are taking the weight of boom, sail, and gaff.

First-reef earing ⅜": from stopper knot under boom cheek port side, up through leach cringle, down through dumb sheave in cheek starboard side, forward to cleat on boom. (Second reef earing is within reach from the deck and can be simply lashed.)

Main sheet ⅜": from becket on traveller block, up through front-shackle block on boom sling, down through traveller block, up through two front shackle blocks on boom slings, down to 8" cleat in cockpit.

Jib sheets (two) ¼": straight from clew of sail to belaying pins port and starboard.

Jib furling line ¼": from around drum on tack swivel aft around corner of companionway shroud to deck cleat port side (not shown).

No standing rigging; no wire except in luff of jib.

19

MONHEGAN

$18'0'' \times 7'0'' \times 3'6''$

A Friendship sloop is a boat built wide, deep, and heavy for her length, with an exaggerated rake to her midsection producing a combination of sharp bow and powerful quarters. The special forte of such boats is weatherliness; they're not particularly fast to windward and have a low maximum speed (that is, they're slow reaching) but a lot more wind and sea are required to smother them than most boats can stand. That's not the same thing as seaworthiness; a Friendship with a big open cockpit and a heap of loose scrap iron or rocks for ballast is obviously not seaworthy by modern standards no matter how weatherly she is.

The *Monhegan* design calls for a very strong deck and foot well, plus such small matters as ventilators on the centerline, and she's specially laid out from scratch to use inside iron set in concrete. Besides being cheap and simple to arrange, this has some real functional advantages, among others that you never have the condition of the keel bolts on your mind. Loose inside ballast will destroy a boat in short order unless it's carried inside a heavy ceiling, in which case it can't be stowed decently low and is apt to shift when you need it most, but concrete, if it's well worked into all the odd corners, will usually preserve both the shape and the timber. I'm of an opinion that it's not necessary or even good to paint or tar under the concrete, or that the wood needs to be dry for the pouring, and would be much inclined to pour with the boat afloat so she can be trimmed as you go. I took a good deal of trouble figuring the space available, but of course I can't control the mix of metal and concrete very well, to say nothing of other unguessable weights that turn up on stock designs.

Besides being relatively free of what Claud Worth called "morbid anxiety about the weather," a boat of this type has an advantage at the other end of the spectrum: with her deep, easy bow, great momentum, and long-boomed gaff rig, she's much better able to cope with the plague of motorboat wakes in light weather than lighter boats with more modern-looking

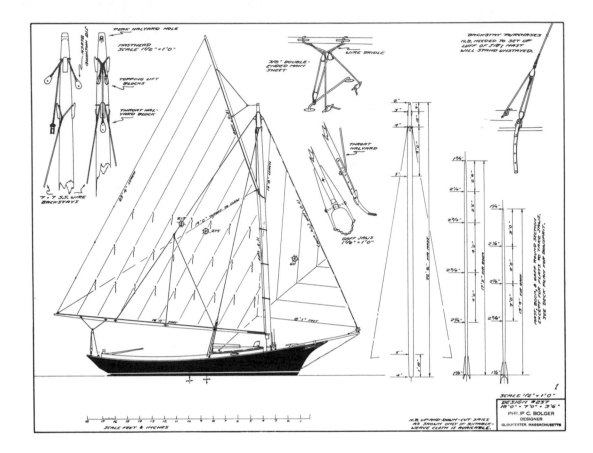

rigs. As long as she's not pinched, she's a first-class ghoster. She has a very big rig for her size; the size of the boat is so small that such a rig doesn't create any problems in relation to a man's strength, but now and again it will help her surprise some more racy type in light and moderate weather.

There is no room for sleeping berths or any way to get them in without spoiling her good looks. The cuddy is for locked stowage, for decency with a chemical toilet, and to make it possible to get at the engine, if she has one, and start it or work on it without leaving her all open to the weather. An engine placed like this one might be some good to you in a rough lee shore situation.

Short beamy boats with counter sterns are never the most convenient to frame and plank, but I've tried to match up the sectional shape with the sheer line so that the upper planks will lie naturally. This eliminates the usual elliptical transom, but it ought to keep the sheer from going flat aft as it does in too many Friendships. This ought to be a very pretty boat indeed.

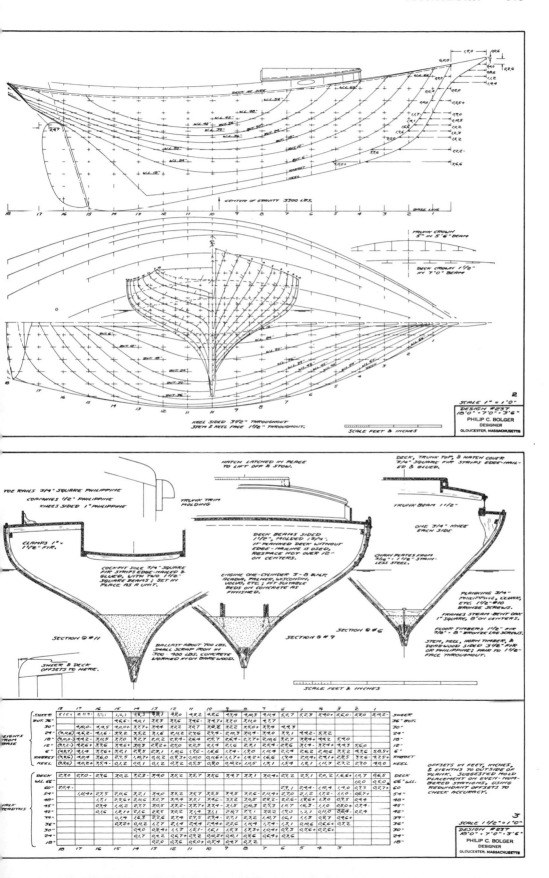

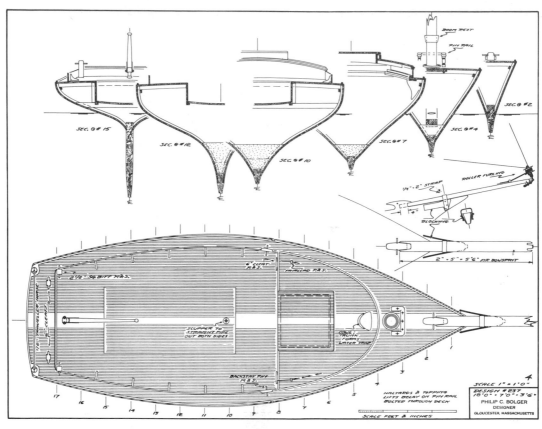

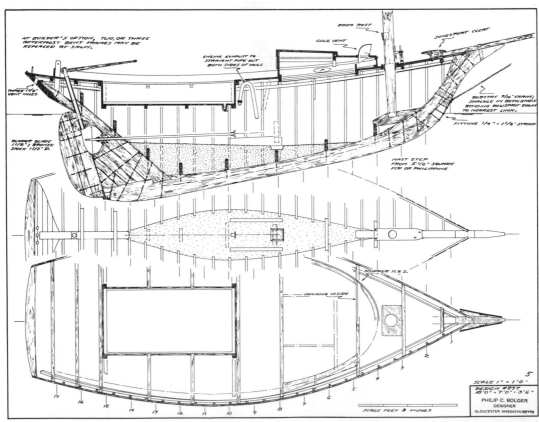

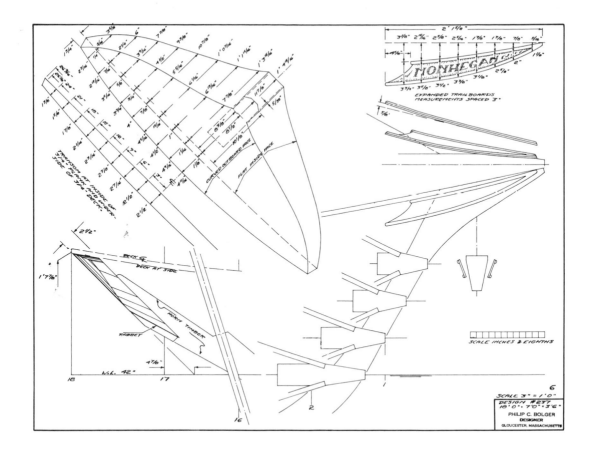

EXPANDED TRAILBOARDS
MEASUREMENTS SPACED 3"

MONHEGAN

SCALE INCHES & EIGHTHS

SCALE 3" = 1'0"
DESIGN #277
19'0" · 7'0" · 3'6"
PHILIP C. BOLGER
DESIGNER
GLOUCESTER, MASSACHUSETTS

20

MASTER HAND

22'6" x 18'9" x 7'11" x 4'0"

Between *Master Hand* and *Monhegan* I designed eighty-five boats and would
like to think I'd learned something in the process. I do think the later
design is a neater and more finished job, her model more graceful and behavior more spirited. But I can't say I'm ashamed of the older design; it
has most of the same characteristics, but was designed to be rugged and
powerful, and as nearly indestructable as a small boat can be. She is very
heavy; the construction is massive for her size, the ballast keel very heavy and
carried low. Her rig is not as large in proportion to *Monhegan's*. I haven't
had any report on the sailing of these boats, but I take it they're on the
stodgy side in light airs and wet in a breeze, but stand up on their feet and
punch along in heavy weather in a way few people are used to now.

This is about the smallest boat which can look like a Friendship and still
have something usable as a cabin. The drawings look as if I'd spent a lot
of time trying to get the most out of what space is there, and it seems to me
that a singlehander could make himself pretty comfortable. The cutting
off of the motor from the cabin by a solid bulkhead is to me a great luxury,
and now that it is possible to buy workable portable toilets, one could be
rid of that other unpleasant companion below; the cedar bucket is done for,
not socially responsible any longer on the crowded coasts, but its sophisti-
cated successor has some of its advantages.

She could stand a higher rig, as much as two or three feet more mast and
two feet longer gaff in most waters, I should think, and that much without
any increase in mast diameter; but in some places where it blows hard
habitually, or if you like to minimize panic parties and don't mind giving
the engine frequent use, there's a case to be made for short rigs. I would
now abolish the plank gaff because I find it ugly and inconvenient to stow,
substituting a round one about 2½" diameter in the middle and tapered
to 1½" at each end. A diagram is attached of the altered jib lead I would
use now; with this she'll be faster and closer-winded, enough so to warrant

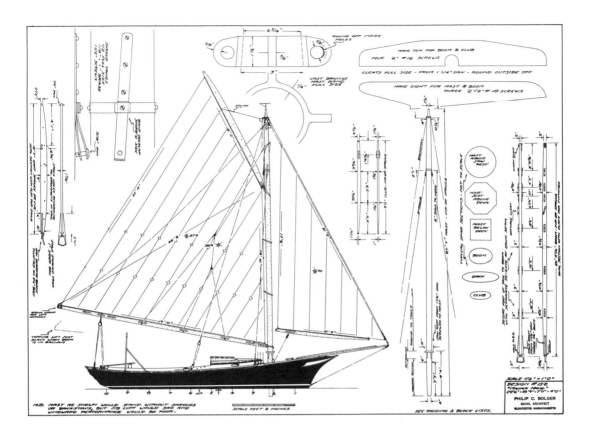

the added complexity and more frequent jams and foulings, in my opinion, though there are people whose judgment I respect who differ on this. A balanced club jib, as shown with the *Featherwind* design, has the advantages of both arrangements, but most people find that it doesn't set as well in strong winds.

I would raise the well flat at least three and probably four inches higher than it is shown; that is, the well would be that much shallower. That will bring it seven or eight inches above the designed waterline, which is a much better margin than four inches against overloading incidents; it will also hold less weight of water if she ships a green sea.

Lastly I would give some thought to making the ballast casting shorter, down to perhaps five and a half feet long from nine feet as designed. I suspect her of being overloaded with ballast as designed, and the sheer weight and size of the casting is daunting to any amateur and many professionals now. One man who built one of these cast her keel in a wooden mold set flush in packed earth; not a bad idea, but a seam cracked on the mold from the heat of the lead, and opened about a sixteenth of an inch. Upwards of two thousand pounds of lead ran through that crack, and, digging down to retrieve the lead, he was still finding bits of it over six feet deep in hard ground. So he said and I don't doubt him. I think the boat has power to spare, and would be drier and livelier if the keel was eight hundred or a thousand pounds lighter and more concentrated amidships.

KEY TO PLAN

1.   Keel sided 3½", maximum molded width about 7¾" oak.
2.   Stem and knee, sternpost and horn timber, etc., sided 3¾" oak; ⅜" bronze bolts.
3.   False keel fairing blocks oak bolted to main keel and ballast casting with ⅜" bronze bolts.
4.   Lead casting about 2,800 pounds; ten ⅝" bronze bolts through floor timbers, two single bolts at each end, three pairs amidships.
5.   Heel timber sided 3¾" oak; three 8" lag screws to keel; rudder heel cup lined with bronze for bearing.
6.   Mast step oak shaped from about 6" x 9" x 3' 9"; lags to stem knee and floor timbers, drain hole through bottom.
7.   Oak base block for marine toilet; drain limber holes under it each side of keel; toilet may be concealed under a removable box.
8.   Rudder blade 1½" oak with ¼" drift rods; fair in trailing edge to about ¾" face; stock 1½" diameter bronze in lead or copper tube through horn timber and deck block; top of stock to take tiller fitting like Merriman #483A and mahogany tiller tapered from 1" x 3" x about 3'.
9.   Transom edge-nailed and glued cedar strips 1¼" square with 1½" oak fastening frame inside; a carved eagle of about 30" wingspan is to be placed on outside of transom to take the curse off its flatness.
10.   After bulkhead ½" fir plywood with 8" diameter deck plate in center and 9" diameter hole each side for ventilation, exhaust, etc.; fastening and stiffening frame ¾" oak.
11.   Main bulkhead ½" with ¾" frame is to be watertight, without drain limbers; this is the only place in the boat where drainage is to be interrupted, the object being to keep engine smell and explosives out of the cabin.
12.   For'd bulkhead same as the others but is partial, cut away under the deck near centerline as shown; this and the other two bulkheads are intended to keep the hull from straining when driven hard and should not be left out, or moved much.
13.   Cockpit sole ½" fir plywood; 1½" x 2½" oak beams; sole fiberglass sheathed with sheathing carried over covings up sides and ends to deck.
14.   Sides of cockpit ½" fir plywood with 1½" x 2½" oak or fir headers under deck and 1" x 2½" oak or fir riser to take cockpit sole and beams; note that these sides carry the cockpit sole between bulkheads and that the whole structure should be well fastened and glued without holidays, as the cockpit could conceivably hold as much as 1,400 pounds of water; to keep the sea in a gale it would be well if the cockpit were smaller and shallower.

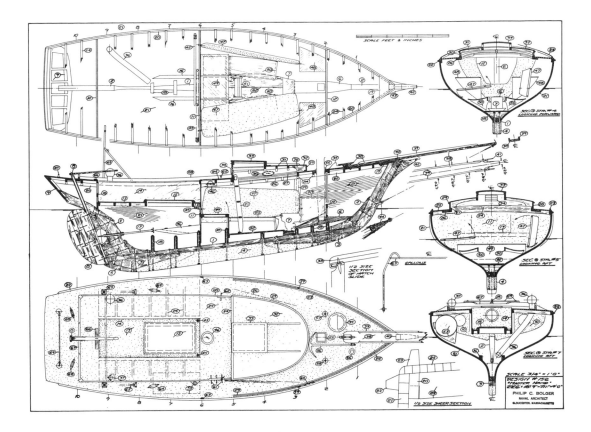

15. Engine hatch ½″ fir plywood on oak or fir frame and coaming, with continuous hinge across for'd edge and a secure latch aft.

16. Engine beds sided 2½″ oak, shaped to fit closely against inside of hull and secured with lags to floor timber at for'd end, and with glue and long screws through from outside of planking aft. Shape will vary with engine selected.

17. Propeller shaft 1″ bronze or Monel with bronze stuffing box and stern bearing; engine used should not be more than 25 h.p. direct drive to a two-bladed propeller not more than 10″ diameter. Palmer IH-60 heavy-duty, 16 h.p. @ 2400 rpm, is suggested, with 10″ diameter by about 6″ pitch Michigan Auxiliary-type two-blade prop; exhaust taken up and aft starboard side to an elbow or vertical silencer abaft after bulkhead, with tailpipe and cooling water outlet passing through transom low and near centerline. *Note:* this boat will sail well enough and carry her way in stays in a fashion to make the engine unnecessary; her sailing would be improved as well as cost reduced if the engine were not installed and the propeller aperture plugged; she could be rowed or sculled easily for short distances.

18. Floor timbers sided 2½″ oak, eight in all, with large limber holes.

19. Breasthook sided 1½″ oak with ⅜″ bolt through stem.

20. Clamps 1″ x 2½″ oak or fir.

21. Planking full 1″ cedar stripping (may be milled hollow and round) glued and edge-nailed, laid up inside external molds.

22. Guard moldings bevelled from 1¼″ x 1½″ oak (broad side fast to hull) with ¾″ outboard face shod if desired with aluminum or bronze half-oval.

23. Toe rails bevelled from 1¼″ x 1½″ oak (short side fast to deck) with ¾″ top face.

24. Deck beams sided 1½″, molded 2½″ oak; 12″ and as shown on centers.

25. Deck ¾″ cedar strips laid straight fore and aft or as convenient, glued and edge-nailed and sheathed with fiberglass carried under coaming and trunk side and turned down under guards.

26. Deck block 1¼″ fir or oak carries deck and beams between full length beams at stations #3 and #5.

27. Inner coaming 1″ square oak or fir sprung to outline of inside of trunk and continued to a sawn padding for'd of station #3 around inside of for'd end of trunk.

28. Coaming sided ¾″ oak steamed or boiled to bend around for'd end of trunk; provide drain hole in coaming at low point of deck in way of cockpit.

29. Trunk trim molding bevelled from ¾″ square oak; across after end of trunk a sawn ½″ oak coaming projecting slightly above trunk top.

30. Fixed lights ¼″ plate glass set in trunk sides.

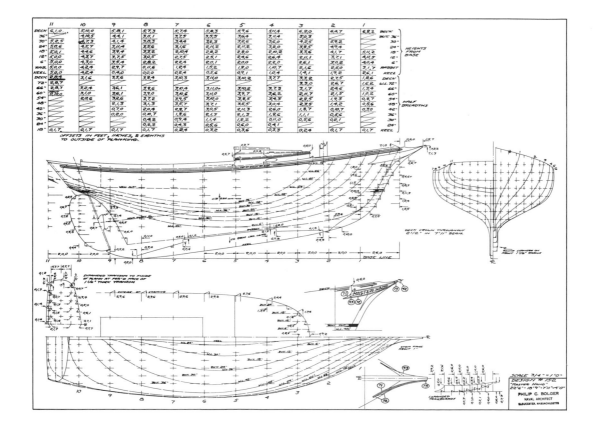

31. Trunk beams sided 1½", molded about 1¾" oak.

32. Trunk top ½" fir plywood sheathed with fiberglass turned under trim moldings.

33. Sliding hatch double ⅜" fir plywood, with 1¼" oak rails.

34. Louvered and screened vent opening in after end of trunk below slide.

35. Sudbury Skyvent or similar watertrap vent, about 12" opening, screened.

36. Turbine vent, about 4" inside diameter, ducted to draw from bilge under engine.

37. Cowl vent, swivelling type, about 3" inside diameter of neck.

38. Bowsprit from 1½" x 9" fir or oak, with oak mooring cleat bolted through deck blocking, four ¼" bolts through deck beams and breasthook, and end fitting of doubled ⅛" x 2" bronze strapping spread to take bobstay pin and secured with two 3" round-head screws to end grain of spar.

39. Bowsprit stiffening cleats 1" x 1½" oak or fir tapered down for'd to about 1".

40. Bowsprit strap ¼" x 3" x 18" bronze or galvanized; four 3" screws on each side, staggered, to stem.

41. Anchor chocks oak bolted through bowsprit and well rounded-off to lead smoothly.

42. False head sided 3¾" oak or fir with 6" lags to stem; fair in below trail-

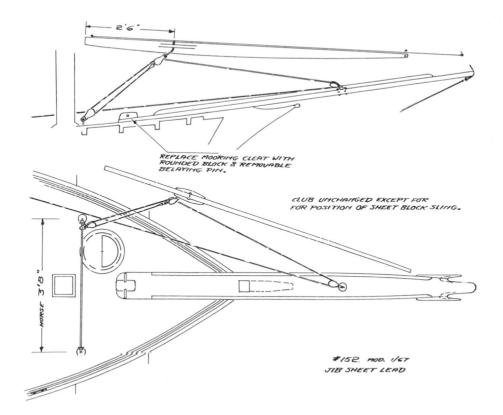

REPLACE MOORING CLEAT WITH
ROUNDED BLOCK & REMOVABLE
BELAYING PIN.

CLUB UNCHANGED EXCEPT FOR
FOR POSITION OF SHEET BLOCK SLING.

#152 MOD. 1/67
JIB SHEET LEAD

boards to about 1″ rounded face; see lines drawing and specifications #71-73 for trailboards; figurehead to taste but should not be much larger than the unicorn head sketched or the scroll indicated on the construction plan.

43. Trail knees sided 1½″ oak or fir, to fit tightly to hull, stem, and trailboards, glued and screwed in place and scuppered to hold no water.

44. Bobstay stem fitting two 3/16″ x 2″ x 18″ bronze or galvanized straps rivetted through stem, with ½″ diameter pin for bobstay.

45. Lead tube cockpit scuppers with bronze through-hull fittings and seacocks; note scuppers cross, port side of cockpit to starboard side of hull and vice versa, not less than 1½″ inside diameter.

46. Spherical compass in gymbals under 8″ diameter deadlight in deck; paint area round compass under deck white or silvery to reflect light onto compass from lamp placed below and to one side.

47. Pipe berths steel or aluminum tubing; laced canvas bottoms; overall fabric sheath for appearances' sake; berth pivot on extension round bars turning in holes in bulkhead and forward lockers, to form seat backs or berths as shown.

48. Plywood lockers with tight-fitting loose tops, drain holes and low point.

49. Locker with hinged top in three panels; could be built as ice box at considerable expense and rot hazard.

50. Seats ½″ fir plywood sprung to curve athwartships, secured to knee at forward end and to cleat on locker front.

51. Mahogany ladder hung on brackets to be easily removed and put out on deck when cabin is occupied.

52. Floorboards ¾″ teak or rift-grain fir, laid loose.

53. Fuel tank 30 gallon, 16″ diameter by 36″ length or smaller, Allcraft Monel or similar, resting in sawn cleats on bulkhead and on shims aft, and strapped in place to be safe if boat is bottom up or standing on her stern; fill pipe chocked up above deck level outside coaming; fuel line with shutoff at tank end, vent piped aft to through-hull fitting near top of transom. A similar watertank may be placed on the port side if wanted.

54. Coaming of trunk end ¾″ mahogany; a good place for some carving.

55. Mast partner 1½″ oak extends about 21″ to each side; mast wedges L-shaped as shown, oak, to stay in place yet be fairly easy to drive out from below; adhesive tape mast coat painted to match deck.

56. Kedge anchor about 25 pounds with wood chocks and lashing cleats to suit; rode line feeds to forepeak through 2″ deck pipe.

57. Deck plate for swivel block of jib sheet.

58. Pad eye for standing part of jib sheet.

59. Chain plates ¼″ x 2″ x about 24″ bronze or galvanized with four ¼″ bolts through clamp and reinforcing strap inside hull.

60. Chain plate for halyard blocks ¼″ x 12″ x about 8″ bronze or galvanized bolted through clamp; starboard side only.

61. Belaying pins for halyards oak or brass, set in 1″ oak block inside coaming; stagger height as shown on sail plan.

62. Belaying pin for jib sheet.

BLOCK LIST*

	Location	Number	For rope diameter	Fitting
Main sheet	boom	two	½″	front shackle to ½″ rope strop round boom
Main sheet	horse	one	½″	side shackle to horse
Main clew outhaul	boom end	one	¼″	cheek block
Peak halyard	masthead	one	⅜″	upset side shackle to mast band
Throat halyard	hounds	one	⅜″	side shackle— ½″ rope strop round mast seized at block end.
Jib halyard	masthead	one	⅜″	side shackle— ½″ rope strop over mast band seized at block.
Jib sheet	club	one	¼″	side shackle— ⅜″ rope strop round club seized at block.
Jib sheet	deck port side	one	¼″	swivel deck plate
Backstays	purchase	two	⅜″	front shackle
Backstays	purchase	two	⅜″	upset side shackle to chain plates
Halyard deck leads	chain plate starboard side	three	⅜″	upset side shackle with becket

*All single bronze blocks for rope.

RIGGING LIST

	Length	Diameter	Material	One End	Other End
Bobstay	8′ 1″	9/32″	7 x 7 wire	splice around pin	splice around pin
Headstay	24′ 5″	9/32″	7 x 7 wire	7/16″ turnbuckle	splice to shackle
Shrouds (2)	18′ 4″	9/32″	7 x 7 wire	7/16″ turnbuckles	splice around tang pins
Backstays (2)	22′ 3″	3/16″	7 x 7 wire	splice to shackle	splice to block
Backstay purchases (2)	16′	½″	manila	splice to block becket	stopper knot
Main sheet	80′	½″	manila or nylon	stopper knot	stopper knot
Main clew outhaul	3′ 6″	¼″	manila	stopper knot	whip
Topping lift	28′ 6″	⅜″	nylon	splice to shackle	eye splice around mast
Lazyjacks (2)	see sail plan	¼″	nylon	Eye splices around mast, thimbles and stopper knots as shown.	
Peak halyards	54′	⅜″	manila	eye splice around gaff	stopper knot
Throat halyard	42′	⅜″	manila	eye splice around gaff	stopper knot
Jib halyard	54′	⅜″	manila	bend to head cringle	stopper knot
Jib sheet	30′	¼″	nylon	bend to pad eye	stopper knot
Anchor rode	200′	½″	nylon	bend to anchor	bend around mast step

63. Chain plates for backstay purchase blocks ¼″ x 2″ x 18″ bolted through clamp and straps inside hull.

64. Backstay cleats about 8″ oak jamming type bolted through blocks under deck.

65. Gallows fabricated from ¾″ standard pipe galvanized after forming and welding; weld into sockets and bolt through blocks under deck.

66. Comb oak or mahogany with radial slots to take ⅛″ brass blade set in underside of tiller.

67. After end of coaming 1¼″ oak, cut down in way of tiller swing.

68. Main sheet cleats about 8″ oak cut high and well-rounded for free veering; bolt-through blocks under deck.

69. Main sheet horse galvanized, fitted with adjustable traveller stops, and bolted through blocks under deck. *Note:* inaccessible bolts should be pinned or otherwise secured against unscrewing.

70. Oak trunk knee sided about 1¼″ on centerline.

71. Trailboards ½″ mahogany sprung on and screwed to trail knees, hull, and false stem; may be carved in shallow relief or painted to taste.

72. Trim moldings ½″ square mahogany.

73. End block of trim moldings ½″ thick each side.

Note to builders: use judgment as to materials; designer approves use of hard pine or Philippine instead of oak and similar variations according to local good practice; solid timbering may be replaced with laminations at will.

21

VANITIE

19′8″ x 15′0″ x 5′11″ x 3′0″

About 1918, Montgomery Boat Yard built a class of eighteen or twenty sloops called the Annisquam Bird Class, designed by the late Harry Friend and Nicholas Montgomery. They were built with centerboards but changed over to shoal keels after a year or two, and made a great reputation for speed and rough water ability. If you can imagine the *Mouser* catboat in this book stretched out longer, narrower, and much lower, you'll have a fair idea of their model.

No more of them were built, and by the time the class had been raced for fifty years the ones still sailing were looking quite tired. Erik Ronnberg had admired them for years, and took a notion to have the Montgomery yard build him a new boat for day-sailing in Sandy Bay, around the corner from Annisquam. They no longer had any usable molds or plans for the Birds, but a model was unearthed which apparently represented a modified Bird especially intended for Sandy Bay, where the water is deeper and the winds tend to be lighter than at Annisquam. The model showed a hull with a much longer entrance and shorter run, more deadrise and rocker, and a deeper fin, in general more graceful and less powerful, than the Birds. Erik had me draw plans based on this model, with various minor modifications, such as putting the rudder stock more upright and giving her just enough concavity in the sheer to avoid a hogged look. Between us we devised a gaff rig that seemed suited to the hull, as the original sail plan was missing.

To my mind, a one-off boat this size needs a lot of justifying, as it's highly unlikely that whatever you do will turn out to be a big enough improvement over some existing class to warrant the trouble. However, if you want a day-sailer suitable for being sailed singlehanded in a relaxed fashion, but still light and fast, there's not much offered. Sandy Bay is the home of a strong fleet of Stars, but the Star is no singlehander; I was crew in one for some years and frequently wished there were two of me. The obvious choice

Vanitie *with one reef in her main*

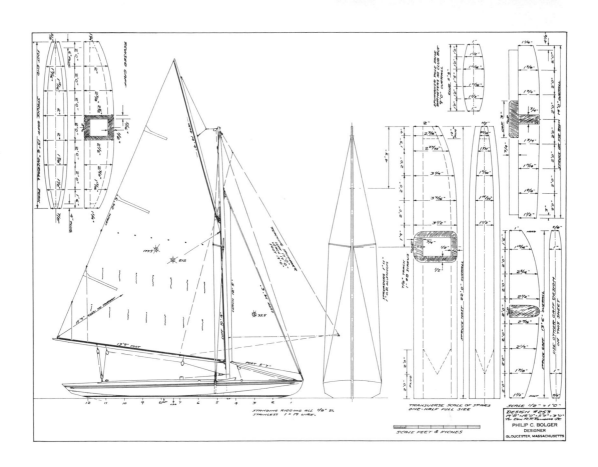

would be an International 110 and that is a design I always admired very much myself, but they are a little dull in light airs and Erik did not care for their looks or the plywood construction.

So *Vanitie* was built. Erik is one of the top industrial and historical model-makers in business and took pains with the detail and finish, producing the beautifully shaped tiller and Jonesport cleats, special rope-stropped wood-shell blocks, and all kinds of little niceties, some drawn on the plans from his specification, some not. She had nothing but the best: Honduras mahogany and Burma teak, all bronze fastenings, spruce spars by Pigeon, dacron sails by Ike Manchester. Partly as a whim and partly for quite practical reasons, almost nothing went into her that wasn't available for the 1918 class, as for instance she has her decks sheathed with cotton duck, a nice material for the purpose if you can get and keep just the right amount of paint on and in it. No plywood was used; no fiberglass; and no glue except in the spars. There is a quite deliberate implication, with which I'm inclined to agree, that the dacron sail is the only new material that's indisputably better than what it replaced. As may be, the whole effect is very

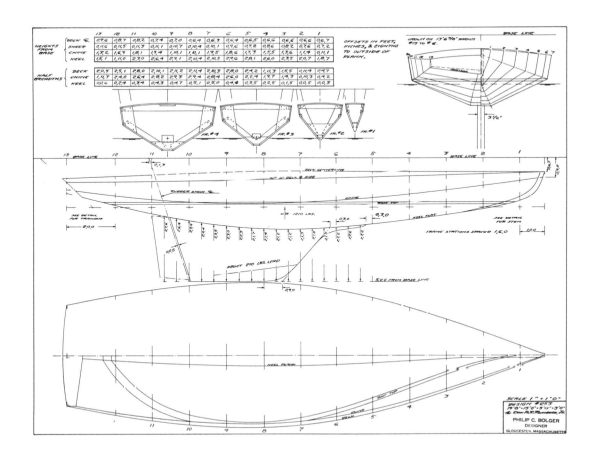

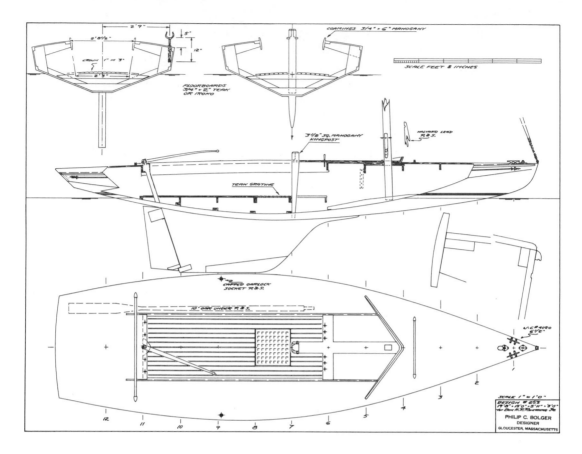

rich and fine, much admired and probably plain cash value in the long run, *if* it's maintained with care, for which you need either a temperament I unfortunately don't have myself or enough "disposable income" to hire it done; neglect of a structure like this is expensive and hard on the conscience.

The lead ballast casting is a very small one, but the big old-fashioned fin is oak and extremely heavy with its bronze bolts. The result is that she's effectively self-righting and immune to being blown over by a squall on her mooring, yet is fully buoyant just from the wood structure without having to add any foam; or if the owner so chose, there's ample room for enough foam to float her very high, even to make it possible to sail her after a fashion completely flooded. Her total weight, with one man and considerable gear, is between 1,100 and 1,200 pounds, just a bit lighter than her designed lines as drawn.

The cockpit turned out very comfortable, the proportions being just right for back and foot braces up to large angles of heel. The slight crown of the sole is typical of the trouble taken with her, its effect on looks being subtle if not negligible, but the effect on seating comfort quite noticeable. Of

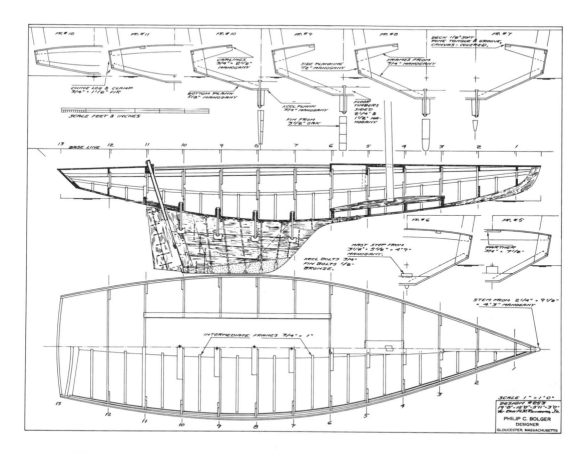

course, if there are two or more people aboard, they generally sit or lie on the deck, and with any weight in the wind she sails much faster if the crew perches to windward and hikes out. The point is that it's not necessary to have the extra crew or to make them hike out, as she will sail, and won't swamp or capsize, when sharply heeled. Moreover, she is fitted with effective topping lifts, lazyjacks, and reefing gear so that reducing sail is convenient to an extent almost unheard-of in boats of her size, and the slim gaff well up on end reduces weight and windage aloft in proportion to the reduction in sail; the special gooseneck for the gaff, running on a track, was designed by L. Francis Herreshoff and allows much better staying and rigging arrangements than the traditional jaws.

Vanitie is a fast boat and a thoroughbred; on her trial trip she sailed eight nautical miles in an hour and a half, a quarter of the distance dead to windward in very rough water, reefed. In crowded places she can be pinched by obstacles, quickly gathering way and carrying it, and in general having all the good manners that could be asked. She's admirable to watch on the wind in a chop as the long hungry bow slices through the crests. Off the wind she also goes very fast, though she's too deep-bodied and doesn't have enough

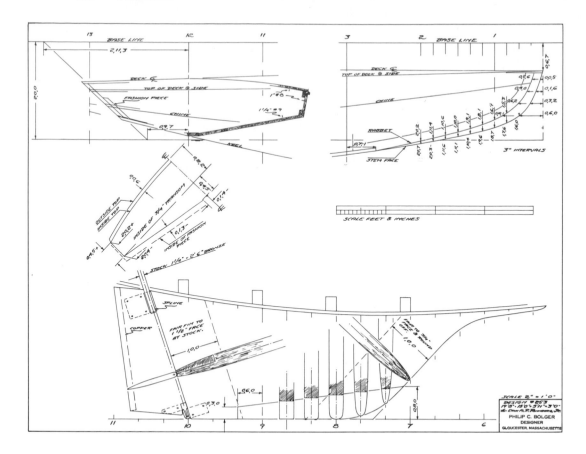

bearing aft to take off and fly in a strong breeze as some centerboarders can.
I suggested when we were designing her that she would be faster if we put
the transom up vertical or with more or less tumblehome, and the stern
would be easier to build and stronger as well; this notion was vetoed on
grounds of appearance; I don't really think it makes any difference to her
behavior that you'd ever notice unless you had two of them with that
difference and no other. She's weatherly, handy, and reliable, and will be
more so as soon as the new gaff, the hollow one drawn on the sail plan, is
added. I cut the old gaff to the bare minimum, as weight saved in that
location is at a high premium per ounce in a boat like this with a big rig
and a hull without great initial stability. The bare minimum in strength
proved not stiff enough: it didn't break, but did develop a compression bend
from the span, and what that does to the set of her pretty mainsail, when
there's some weight in the wind, would make Ike Manchester very sad if he
could see it. Incidentally, *Lynx's* gaff is also a bit more flexible than is
perhaps ideal, but being square it bends mostly the right way and tends to
flatten the sail instead of distorting it. Another half inch of thickness
through most of its length might be warranted, however.

22

OTTER

19'6" x 4'10"

Otter was designed for a high-school senior living on the north shore of Long Island, a good carpenter and the son of a good carpenter. She was designed to be as quickly and cheaply built as possible, including the rig and outfitting as well as the hull, to be used for singlehanded weekend cruising and day-sailing on the Sound. I designed her so that she would be a lively and weatherly sailer able to deal with rough water in a competent fashion, and as safe as a half-decked boat can well be. She won't be an easy boat to swamp. If she is swamped, it is supposed to be possible to right and bail her out while afloat; she can be rigged and unrigged by one person while afloat and without any outside help.

Very few people have designed and sailed as many sharpies as I have, and the boat on which this design is primarily based has been sailing for upwards of fifteen years. I also have had eleven years of personal use of a larger version. I think the proportions indicated are just about optimum for a flat-bottomed, sharp-bowed sailing hull; the seemingly excessive rocker in the bottom is the result of a long series of experiments. I should say that I do not consider sharpies to be good investments as a rule; the savings in construction cost are almost always outweighed by the difficulty of selling them for a fair price, and the larger and more elaborate they are the more certain this is. This one is about as large as I would consider at all at present.

The rig was primarily selected because it does away with special spar stock and with most of the expensive fittings required by conventional sail plans. It is nothing more or less than an old-fashioned cat-schooner with a jigger added, the only innovation being the sharp rake of the foremast which is intended to get some of the weight out of the bow and, more important, to improve the aerodynamics of the mainsail. The masts are all short and light enough to be lifted out and laid flat without much effort or preparation; whether this warrants the specified elimination of tracks and halyards on jib and jigger is a matter of opinion, but I have tried the arrangement and am using it at present in a smaller boat with satisfaction. The principal objection to the rig in this design is that if it's desired to sail her under mainsail alone with the other sails stowed to reduce windage, the only convenient place to stow the other two masts is on the deck forward, projecting some distance out over the bow.

The water ballast is cheap and it's very nice to be able to dump it for transportation and storage. It's about as effective in a hull of this type as metal, the only drawback to it being that it doesn't have the self-righting power when the boat is swamped that lead or iron would have.

The cabin can't be made higher without seriously hurting her sailing ability and incidentally, increasing the number of butts and amount of plywood needed quite a lot. It's a big improvement on a tented open boat for sleeping, while such cooking as you'd expect to do, sitting around, etc., can be done under the tent in the cockpit. The cuddy also provides effective locked stowage.

The leeboard and rudder designs have been tested, except for the drag-link tiller connection, which I've got some qualms about. It may have too much

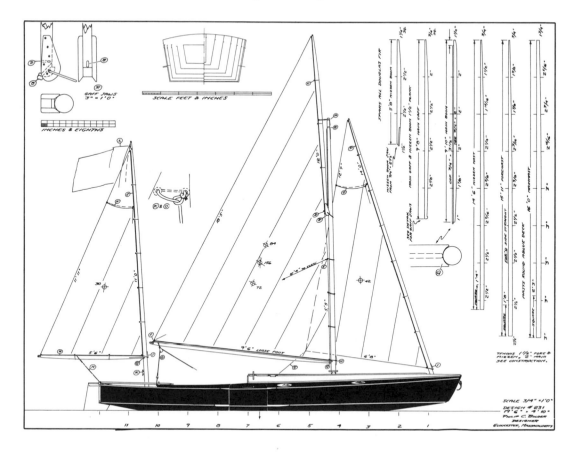

friction to be pleasant to use; if so it can be replaced with a tiller pivotted at the after end of the cockpit and connected to the rudder with two yokes and cables, or by outboard-motor-type cables to a wheel. She would not trim properly if the helmsman sat far enough aft to steer with a conventional tiller. The rudder should be fitted with four gudgeons and a rod through all, rather than with pintles and gudgeons as specified.

The expansions given will be found very accurate, but they are no better than the whole set-up and are worse than useless if the frames are not spaced and plumbed with perfect accuracy; the extremely tight arrangement of components on the plywood sheets could also easily become impossible with a slight distortion or carelessness. The design as presented is laid out to be quick to build by a skilled carpenter rather than easy for a tyro; the latter would probably be well advised to revert to cut-and-try and resign himself to much more wastage of plywood.

KEY TO PLAN

All plywood is from 4' x 8' sheets, thickness as specified; wood not specified as plywood is Douglas fir or equivalent, using standard "dressed lumber" sizes approximating those given. All joints are glued with Borden or other waterproof marine glue; fastenings unless otherwise specified are monel "Anchorfast" nails. If gluing is done without holidays, sheathing is unnecessary, but fiberglass or other plastic sheathing at joints or overall is acceptable.

The expansions given are accurate if the hull is accurately set up with molds plumb and rigid. All dimensions are to outside of plank and to edge before rounding-off, leaving a margin for error averaging about 1/4".

1. Bulkhead with 3/4" x 1 1/2" fastening frame at deck and sides, 3/4" x 3 1/2" at bottom; note notch for stem knee with drainage.

2. Temporary mold from 3/4" x 3 1/2" with scrap plywood gussets; secure deck beam across with screws or bolts; this will be left in place when mold is removed before decking.

3. Bulkhead with opening as shown; deck fastening frame from 3/4" x 2 1/2" (all deck beams and tops of bulkheads have same 8' radius crown), bottom fastening frame 3/4" x 2 1/2" with 1/2" x 1 1/2" drainage cut-outs each side; side fastening frames 3/4" x 1 1/2".

4. Temporary mold similar to #2 except that deck beam is from 4" wide stock and has about 1 1/2" crown on lower edge.

5. Mold legs carry deck beam from 4 3/8" stock with 1 3/4" crown on underside, and bottom frame from 1 1/2" x 2" bevelled on top to take inner bottom #27; no drain or vent holes; note cut-out for end of double bottom shelf #18.

6. Similar to #5, but deck beam is 4 3/4" deep including 2 1/8" crown on underside, and bottom frame is 3/4" x 3 1/4" with drainage cutouts in bottom and vent cutouts in top.

7. Main bulkhead as detailed, side and door frames 3/4" x 1 1/2"; deck frame

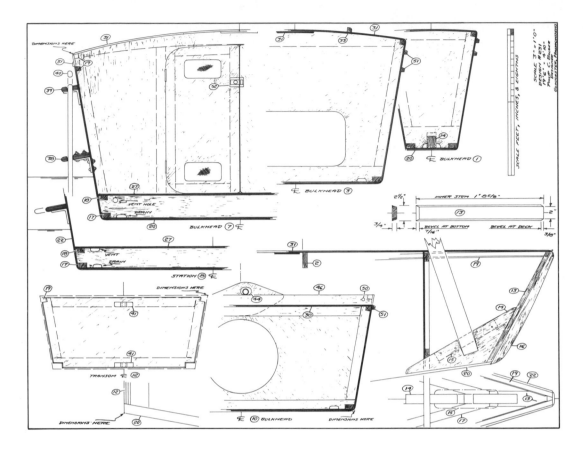

from ¾" x 4¼" with 1⅞" crown on underside; 1½" x 3⅝" bottom frame, doubled forward and aft of bulkhead. Note drainage cutout and ¾" diameter vent hole each side.

8.   Mold legs carry ¾" x 3⅛" bottom frame similar to the one at #6; no deck beam but the legs might be better for a diagonal brace till the planking is on.

9.   Legs carry a bottom frame 1½" fore and aft by 1¼" high with about ¼" bevel to take after end of double bottom; no drains or vents; slot for double bottom shelf.

10.   Bulkhead with hole as shown; ¾" x 1½" fastening frame all round; no crown in deck; see #46, etc.

11.   Temporary mold, no part to be left in after planking, ¾" x 3½" with plywood gussets.

12.   Transom: no opening, no crown; fastening frame ¾" x 1½", ¾" x 2½" across top; note that dimensions are given at after face of transom, outside planking, with resulting deduction of 3/16" plus 3/16" bevel if total thickness is 1"; check against actual thicknesses; deck deduction ¼".

13.   Stem from ¾" x 2½"; see detail for bevel.

14.   Knee 1½" sided, 1'9" long from 5½" wide; cut to form mast step.

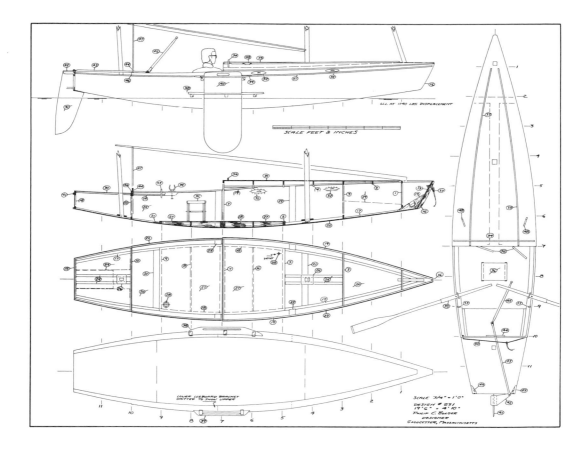

15.   Cheeks of mast step ¾″ x 1½″; four ¼″ bolts through knee.

16.   Stem cap from 1½″ x 2½″ x 1′9″, curved in to ¾″ at top as shown and well rounded all ways.

17.   Chine logs ¾″ x 1½″.

18.   Double bottom shelf ¾″ x 1½″; make sure these lie in a flat plane to take the inside plywood, and that they fit thoroughly watertight at #5, #7, and #9.

19.   Clamp and gunwale stringers from ¾″ square.

20.   Bottom ⅜″ plywood.

21.   Bottom butt straps ¼″ plywood.

22.   Hull sides ¼″ plywood.

23.   Side butt straps ¼″ x 4″ plywood.

24.   Stringers of mizzen mast step ¾″ x 1½″.

25.   Stringers of main mast step 1½″ square.

26.   Main and mizzen mast steps ¾″ plywood.

27.   Inside of double bottom ¼″ plywood in two sections; be very careful with these as seepage of the ballast water would be as annoying as any other leak; make sure that all gaps in the end and side joints are tight or filled, smear the faces with seam compound, and screw down the plywood sheets with about ¾″ bronze screws spaced not more than about 4″; don't use glue and nails here as it

may be desirable at some time to be able to remove the double bottom easily.

28. Flush-screw deck plate about 2½″ opening, like Manhattan G487. To take on ballast water, heel boat slightly to port and trim down by the head; if the drains and vents are clear as designed the double bottom can be filled from this single deck plate without appreciable air pockets, but to pump out without much fiddling with trim, a smaller plate in the opposite corner is desirable for venting. Salt water is best for ballasting, but it is better to have clean fresh water than dirty salt water; about forty-two gallons is the quantity, being 358 pounds of salt or 347 pounds fresh water. If iron or lead ballast is substituted for the water, some such weight should be used and it should be placed in bars laid athwartships next to, and preferably bolted to, the #7 bulkhead; there is no performance advantage in using metal ballast in this hull, but the space saved by it would make bilgewater less of a nuisance.

29. Foam buoyancy: it's suggested that cut blocks, preferably a fairly dense foam, be used rather than an expanding pour-in; note that a clear space is left around the foot of the mizzen mast, and that the lower part of the forward compartment is left clear for stowage, among other things for the ends of the oars; the foam is not supposed to fit so tightly anywhere that condensation water is trapped by it. If the water ballast is used as specified, the boat will be quite

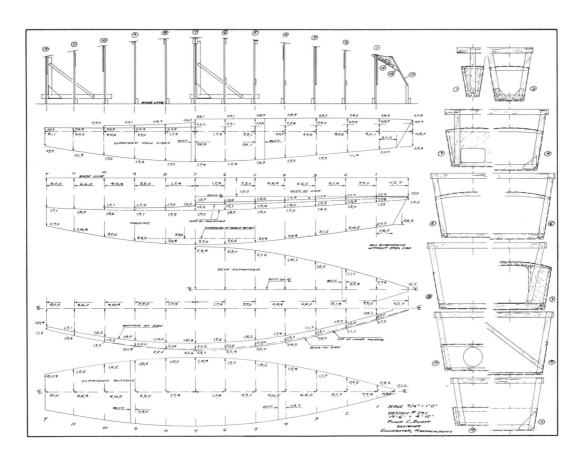

unsinkable without any foam, but with the foam she will be self-righting when swamped and will float high enough when fully swamped to be readily bailed out; the foam is also needed to support the flat afterdeck and that part of it should be fitted well enough to have a good bearing on both deck and bottom.

30. Afterdeck ¼″ plywood.

31. Foredeck ¼″ plywood in three sections, with ¼″ x 4″ butt strap athwartships and ¼″ x 6″ strap fore and aft along the centerline; deck has same crown its full length; no reinforcement at the partners is needed.

32. Deadlights ⅛″ clear plastic screwed to inside of hull.

33. Toe rails ¾″ square, glued to deck and further secured with ⅞″ wood screws driven from below on 3″ to 4″ spacing.

34. Coaming ¾″ x 1½″ sprung over crown.

35. Rowlock mounting blocks ¾″ thick; rowlocks any standard type; oars eight-foot straight-blade spruce or ash.

36. Folding camp stool for rowing seat; 13½″ height shown should be about right, but check for comfort before cutting legs.

37. Bronze shoulder eye bolt ⅜″ x 3½″; splice in, with thimble, about ½″ dacron pennant 12′ long with free end spliced to a belaying T; the idea is that the anchor is dropped from the cockpit and enough scope paid out; then belay

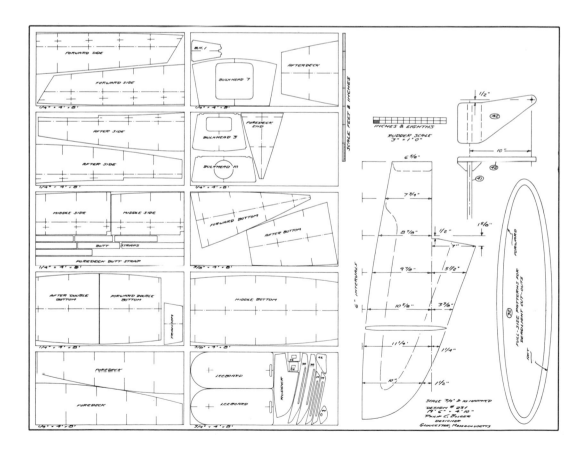

to T and slack out till strain comes on the pennant; hence, no chafe.

38.   Lower leeboard brackets four feet long ¾″ plywood sawn to fit against curve of hull side, secured with three galvanized angles each about ¼″ x 2″ x 2½″ x 2½″, with ¼″ bolts as shown; large washers inside hull; slot to take leeboards a loose fit, taking pains to get slots parallel with hull centerline; do *not* toe in slots for alleged airfoil effect.

39.   Upper leeboard brackets similar but three feet long and with only two supporting brackets each.

40.   Leeboards ¾″ plywood, about 2′0″ x 4′5″, with handhold as shown and a stop to prevent dropping through upper slot; also a removable pin to prevent floating up when heeled. Sharpen leeboard edges about as shown for the rudder.

41.   Rudder blade ¾″ plywood, see drawing for dimensions and fairing; standard bronze pintles and gudgeons like Manhattan G1116 & 1117.

42.   Tiller arm ¾″ plywood, screwed down on 1½″ square cheeks or metal angles each side of blade.

43.   Tiller drag link about 1″ outside diameter aluminum tube flattened out each end.

44.   Drag link guide hole in ¾″ plywood flat.

45.   Extension arm from 1″ round wood with snap fitting on end to engage drag link, like Manhattan G902.

46.   After cockpit coaming ¾″ x 1½″.

47.   Crutches each side, one for foremast as shown, the other for the boom, both to support a cockpit tent.

48.   Six-inch wood cleats for foresail sheets.

49.   Pierced blocks for mizzen sheets.

50.   Traveller horse ⅜″ dacron rope, ends knotted inside coaming.

51.   Trim moldings from ½″ x ¾″, section about as shown; cut back in way of leeboards as necessary.

52.   Cuddy doors, each with screened vent opening top and bottom; catch or lock to suit.

53.   Belaying pins for mizzen sheets ¾″ square.

54.   A big cleat on centerline, set athwartships over the #9 frame, might be best for the fall of the main sheet, though not shown.

Sail plan

Note: All lines ¼″ diameter dacron. All spars Douglas fir of best standard lumberyard stock, as straight-grain and free of knots as can be found; special spar stock is not necessary or very desirable with this cantilever rig, which is why she is a schooner rather than a yawl.

A.   Peak halyard spliced around gaff, lead through well-rounded hole in masthead and down to belaying pin on mast just above deck.

B.   Throat halyard held by stopper knot through hole in heel of gaff, up through hole about 6″ below masthead and down to the other belaying pin; these belaying pins should be blocked off the mast far enough to allow the jaws to come around.

C.   Lash head of sail to gaff with separate ties.

D.　Lashing to jaws 9'5" below peak of sail.

E.　Throat of sail and uppermost of three dacron loops loose on mast.

F.　Clew of mainsail lashed tightly to boom.

G.　Main sheet: splice or snap hook to traveller horse, up through block slung on boom, down to hand or to cleat #54.

H.　Cleat screwed to mast to keep mainsail tack lashing from shifting; with tack lashed here and to boom, boom itself needs no parrel or downhaul.

I.　Stops for foresail and mizzen tack lashings.

J.　Luff of mizzen sail lashed to mast with separate ties; head lashing through hole about 5" below mast truck; no halyard.

K.　Brail: standing end a loop with stopper knot on starboard side of a grommet in luff of sail; fall passes through grommet, back on port side of sail, through leach grommet, forward through loop and down to cleat below boom. To furl sail, free sheets, lift boom end, set brail up tight, swing boom up against mast, and put ties round boom, sail, and mast as high as can be reached; mast can then be lifted out and laid down if desired.

L.　Flag halyard passes through hole in mizzen truck.

M.　Lash foot of mizzen sail to boom.

N.　Mizzen sheets separate port and starboard; each spliced around boom, led down through smoothed hole in blocks screwed to corners of stern, and forward under traveller horse to cleats #53.

O.　Foresail brail same as mizzen; foresail should always be lifted out when sail is furled if there is any amount of wind.

P.　Foresail luff lashed to mast same as mizzen, etc.

Q.　Boom jaws just a scoop in end of 3/4" plank; cap of main boom and a short section under mizzen.

R.　Gaff jaws shaped from 3/4" plank screwed to heel of gaff; see quarter-size three-view on sail plan.

S.　Foresail sheets port and starboard single part; would be well to knot the ends through holes in the coaming or elsewhere.

23

ARCHAEOPTERYX

$$15'6'' \times 6'0''$$

This is one of those brainstorm designs that is apt to be too crafty for the designer's good, or anybody else's. Some people who built one report that the tricky assembly method does work, and that it sails very fast; whether that justifies the bizarre appearance, and the risk that some slight mismeasurement will throw all the inter-related parts into chaos, is up to each individual.

The root of the idea lay in the reluctance of amateurs and one-off builders in general to do their homework on lofting. By the method explained here, if the plywood parts are cut out accurately to the given shapes and put together in the specified order, the hull must come out to the designed shape without any cut-and-try fudging. In fact, it did so the one time it was tried, and only two mistakes were noted. First, the bottom skids #20 and the center shoe #21 ought not to be attached before bending the bottom sheet and fastening it in place; with the chine logs on the other side the bend turns out to be too stiff and the skid fastenings over-stressed; these stringers, which are only needed to protect the plywood from wear, should be put on after the hull is closed in and the screws that can't be driven from outside eliminated. Second, the short chain plates #49 are inadequate and ought to be lengthened by eight or ten inches and carried down and in along the seat leg.

As for the design itself, it is of course an attempt to cross the virtues of a sailboard with those of a conventional sailing dinghy, by making a rather large and stiff sailboard type and adding the comparatively comfortable picnic seat, which keeps your bottom out of the damp. The seat also forms a hiking board, giving her a lot of sail-carrying power without much athletic effort on the crew's part. The area it encloses is a little too large to be ideal for a poker table and too small for a Rotary dinner, but no doubt ideas for its use will readily come to mind.

Would-be sharpie designers can afford to study the hull form. Almost all

*An Archaeopteryx
drifting near Detroit*

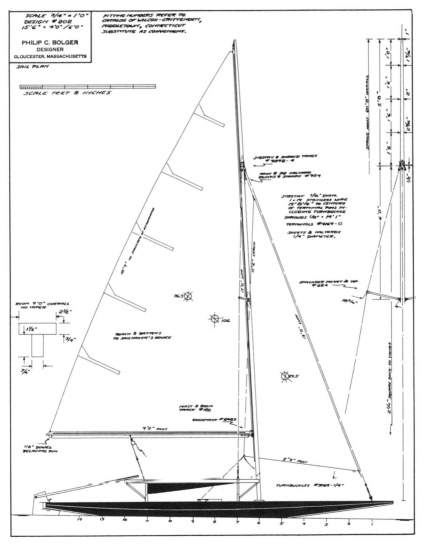

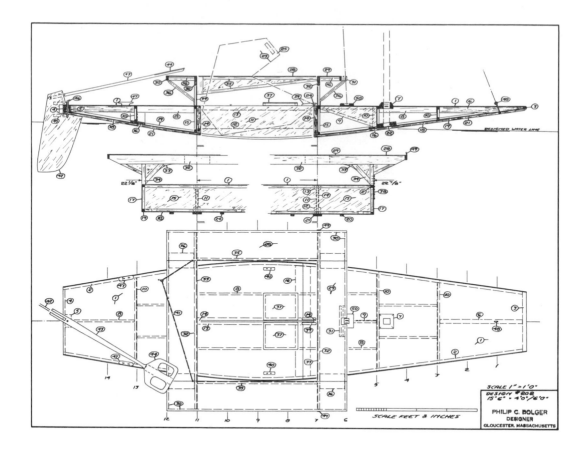

flatbottom boats are designed too straight along the bottom in profile, with the result that they have problems with water eddying under the chine. This shape with the curve of the bottom matched to that of the sides has a reasonably smooth flow pattern, and although the rocker looks exaggerated, it won't stop her from getting up to very high speeds. She will also sail at least as well heeled as upright, which saves considerable effort in puffy winds.

The references to a short mast #7 and #22 concern a version with a sprit rig using a four-dollar bedsheet for a sail; it worked but nobody liked it and I've eliminated the drawing.

KEY TO PLANS

Plywood: all ¼″ exterior-grade Douglas fir 4′ x 8′ sheets except rudder and butt straps; if 16′ sheets are available or smooth scarphs can be produced, eliminate butts.

Natural wood: any of the usual boat-building timbers; sizes given are supposed to correspond to standard dressed lumber dimensions and may vary slightly as

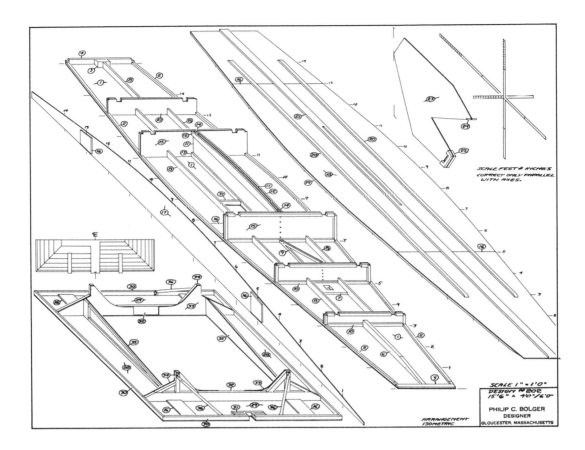

SCALE FEET & INCHES
CORRECT ONLY PARALLEL
WITH AXES.

SCALE 1" = 1'0"
DESIGN #202
15'6" x 40'/6'0"

PHILIP C. BOLGER
DESIGNER
GLOUCESTER, MASSACHUSETTS

ARRANGEMENT
ISOMETRIC

convenient. Moderately hard woods like Douglas fir and Philippine mahogany are preferred to very soft woods like spruce or very hard woods like oak; oak also has poor gluing characteristics.

Screws: about four gross of ¾″ #7 bronze flat-head wood screws; about three dozen 1½″ #10 screws are needed for ends of deck stiffeners and for fastening through shoe to centerboard case, etc.; thirty-two 1″ #8 round-head screws for platform chain plates. Screws are specified instead of Anchorfast or other nails because the slimmer nails tend to sheer off under the stresses of plywood structures; if the gluing is well done, however, usually the nails serve well enough.

1.   Deck cut from two sheets of plywood; secure butt making sure that butt straps stop, leaving room for clamps and centerboard case.

2.   Clamps ¾″ x 1″ bent and secured in place under deck; leave space at one end for the bow block #3.

3.   Bow block 11/16″ x 1½″ x 15 3/16″.

4.   Stern transom ¾″ x 2⅛″ x 27″.

5.   Rudder block 2″ x 2½″ x 5″.

6.   Forward centerline stringer 1½″ x 2½″; stop clear of #3 bulkhead and taper at forward end to take bottom sheet.

7.   Partner block for short mast eliminated.

8.   Deck stiffeners $3/4''$ x $2^1/2''$ from bulkhead to bulkhead, not cut through bulkheads and need not notch over bulkhead fastening frames; two screws at each end of each stiffener $1^1/2''$.

9.   Triangular brace to take thrust of mast, $1/4''$ plywood with $3/4''$ x $1''$ fastening frame.

10.   Bulkheads at stations #3, #5, and #13; $1/4''$ plywood with $3/4''$ x $1''$ fastening frames; note that fastening frames are cut completely for the drainage openings and are not fastened to clamps or chine logs; bulkhead at #5 is screwed through the plywood only, not the fastening frame, to the mast brace; note that bulkheads at stations #5 and #13 are in the way of the bottom and side butt straps and have less contact with clamps and chine logs in consequence; the true dimensions are as follows: #3 — $53/4''$ x $33^1/4''$ with cutouts for chine and clamp $3/4''$ x $1''$; #5 — $8^1/2''$ x $383/4''$ with chine cutouts $1/2''$ x $3/4''$; #13 — $7''$ x $355/8''$ with cutouts as in #5; all have $1/8''$ — plus bevel on sides and bottom, no bevel on top (deck) edge.

11.   Sides of centerboard case $1/4''$ plywood.

12.   Lower fastening frame of case sides $3/4''$ x $3^1/2''$, sawn to profile.

13.   Upper fastening frames of case sides $3/4''$ x $1^1/2''$. (Secure fastening frames to case sides before assembling the two sides on the headblocks.)

14.   Headblocks of case $5/8''$ x $1^1/2''$; assemble case with four $1/4''$ x $3''$ carriage bolts at corners, $3/4''$ screws along plywood ends.

15.   Bulkheads at ends of centerboard case $1/4''$ plywood with $3/4''$ x $1''$ fastening frames as in other bulkheads. (Secure bulkheads to ends of centerboard case with screws through plywood only into headblocks; secure case and bulkhead assembly to underside of deck. Deck should now appear as in the isometric drawing. At this point consider whether blocking is in place on the underside of the deck for anything that may be screwed down on the deck later.)

16.   Butt straps throughout structure $1/2''$ x $6''$; if different, allow for the difference at bulkheads #5 and #13; note that all through, these straps stop at all framing and secure only to the plywood.

17.   Sides $1/4''$ plywood diagramed, sawn out, and assembled from three sections each, as shown. (Bend sides around the deck and bulkhead assembly and secure to clamp and to bulkhead side fastening frames. Sides now hold the deck in a rigid flat plane; deck holds curve of sides; bulkheads prevent sides from twisting.)

18.   Bottom $1/4''$ plywood laid out flat, marked out, cut, and butted as diagramed.

19.   Chine logs $3/4''$ x $1''$ bent around and secured to edges of bottom; note taper at forward ends to clear clamps.

20.   Skids $3/4''$ x $1^1/2''$; see note in text for alteration from drawing.

21.   Center shoe $3/4''$ x $3^1/2''$ with $5/8''$ x $3'9''$ slot for centerboard; see note in text for alteration from drawing.

22.   Step for proposed short mast to be eliminated; see note above. (Look your last on the inside of the hull beyond #7 and #11 bulkheads. Bend bottom assembly over bulkheads, centerboard case, and end blocks, and secure. Note that

it goes inside the edges of the side planks. Hull is now complete and may be primed and painted.)

23.   Centerboard 5/16″ steel; see dimensional diagram; the peculiar shape is intended, among other things, to avoid chattering; if the leading edge can conveniently be well sharpened, it would be an improvement.

24.   Pivot pin of centerboard about ½″ diameter welded to corner.

25.   Handle of board ¾″ wood each side riveted through board and rounded off comfortably.

26.   Item eliminated.

27.   Item eliminated.

28.   Outrigger seat ¼″ plywood 1′0″ wide and 6′0″ long.

29.   Athwartships seats ¼″ plywood 1′0″ x 4′0″.

30.   Border frame ¾″ x 1½″.

31.   Partner for mast built up of three layers of ¾″ x 1½″, with cutout 2½″ wide by 2¼″ deep (there is no strap or fastening needed to hold the mast here).

32.   Main beams ¾″ x 3½″.

33.   Gussets ¼″ plywood.

34.   Posts and braces ¾″ x 1½″ and ¾″ x 1″.

35.   Triangular bracing plates ¼″ plywood with fastening frames ¾″ x 1″.

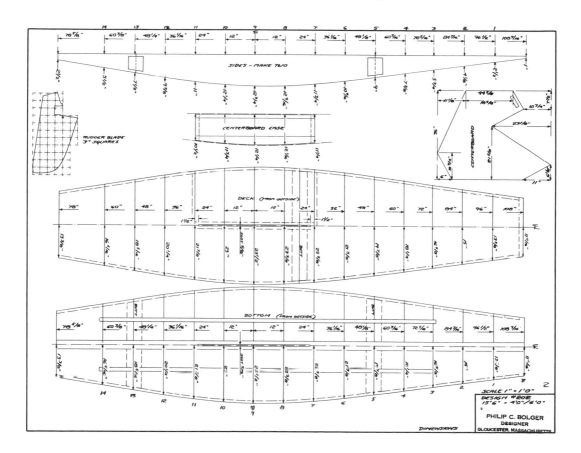

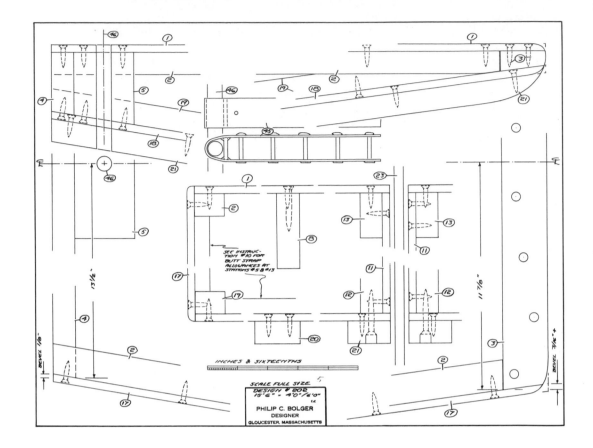

36. Diagonal braces thick-walled aluminum tubing flattened out at ends to take fastenings.

37. Hatches ¼″ plywood, hinged or hooked in place on ¾″ x 1″ frames set on top of deck. Watertight deck plates if preferred, or, on the other hand, open holes with coamings if considerable bailing is acceptable.

38. Seat chain plates about ⅛″ x 1″ x 10″ stainless steel or other metal; four in all with eight 1″ #8 round-head screws each, as shown.

39. Hardwood cleats, open forward, to take centerboard pin.

40. Jib sheet cleats, wood or metal, bolted to the deck with large washers underneath; location is about right for the designed jib.

41. Traveller bridle about ⅜″ rope with stopper knots under seat; traveller is a snap hook on the standing end of the ¼″ sheet; stops may be used if needed, but the lead of the fall should control the boom for the most part.

42. Rudder blade ¾″ plywood; sharpen the leading edge.

43. Tiller from ¾″ x 2½″.

44. Tiller handles ¼″ plywood.

45. Rudder straps steel or brass.

46. Rudder pivot rod about ½″ diameter.

47. Cleats for "cheap rig" sheets may be eliminated.

48. Bronze eye bolt ⅜″ x 4½″.

49. Shroud chain plates about ⅛″ x 1″; see note in text for alteration from drawing.

50. Step from mast ¼″ plywood pad on deck about 6″ square with ¾″ collar; glue to deck and screw to braces #9.

24

QUICKSTEP

| 19'10" x 16'10" x 5'8" x 2'0" |

The history of the Humber canoe yawls (or canoe yachts as some insist they should be called when they reach the size of this one) is scattered in various books. A design for one is in Uffa Fox's *Sailing, Seamanship, and Yacht Construction,* several in *Traditions and Memories of American Yachting* by W. P. Stephens, three or four, including one of the prettiest ever designed, in *The Sailing Boat* by H. C. Folkard, and three in Keble Chatterton's *Fore and Aft Craft.* The best-known example at present is L. Francis Herreshoff's beautiful and fast *Rozinante* class, and this is the one that led to the *Quickstep.*

The man this design was conceived for kept an open day-sailer at the head of a tidal inlet, where he suffered frequently from being kept at anchor, damp and mosquito-plagued, long hours 'till the tide turned or the wind rose. Reading the story of the *Rozinante,* he began to dream of such a boat, but thought she was too deep for his sailing waters, and too long a job for him to build, and asked me to design him a smaller, shallower, and simpler boat. I did so, and he set to work to build her in a way reminiscent of the man who resolved to read *War and Peace* at the rate of one word a day. Some ten years later the hull was completed and he was thinking about doing some joinery and rigging, but in the meantime the state of the world had altered: in the first place, this habitual singlehander met an extraordinarily beautiful girl, married her, and begot three children; in the second place his designer had thought up a large number of things he wished had been done differently in the design.

At his glacial construction pace, his problem, namely how to arrange a singlehander to serve a family of five or more, is not very urgent; I should think the best way to resolve it would be to finish her off with a very large cockpit that can be tented. My reaction to the other half was to make another design to show what I thought I should have done the first time. The new design resembles the first one, but is smaller; the draft is reduced

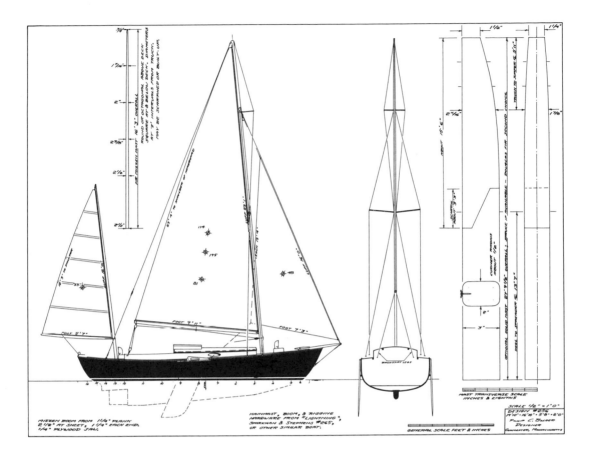

more than her other dimensions and the underwater profile made more
convenient for beaching. Many of the traditional Humber yawls had
underbodies much like this; they were centerboarders, mostly with L-shaped
steel boards placed far forward so that something would be left of the cabin.
I think these boards were badly placed for balance and otherwise not very
good, and the complications of fitting them into the construction can be
fierce, so I concluded to use the dagger leeboards, which besides being much
easier to build and probably more efficient than the small, misplaced, and
contorted centerboards, can be pinned or lashed to serve as legs for grounding out upright. Their only real disadvantage is that, like any surface-
piercing foil, they collect all kinds of floating sculch along the lee side.

Incidentally, she has enough external keel to get around pretty well and
make some progress to windward without the leeboards, but sluggishly
anywhere above a beam reach.

The engine is included because the original design had it, but I'm persuaded it was and is a mistake. For the intended purpose she needed *either*
a cabin in which to smoke and read, and drink, till the flood began to make,

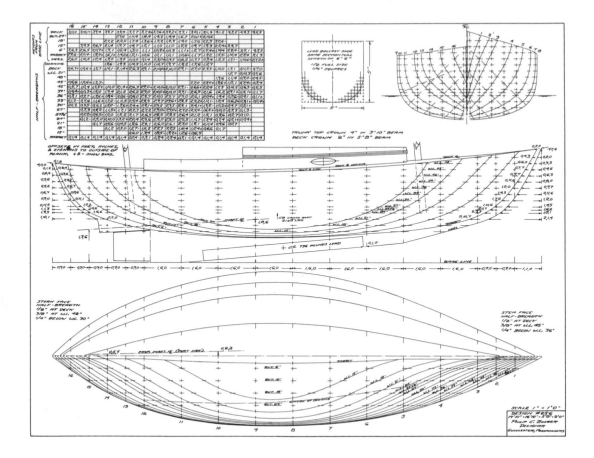

or an engine to fire up and go home regardless, but not, it seems to me, both. In such a situation the tide may make you late getting home, but never more than six hours late. I can't make this possible six hours equal the expense, and complications, and oil in the bilge, and sniffing for gasoline every time you think of lighting a pipe, and general irritation of living with the machine. As may be, there it is, with some notion of how it can be exhausted and ventilated in a fairly satisfactory fashion; it will drive her around six knots and not stop her much under sail; the penalty for the latter good quality being that it won't take much of a head sea to pitch the prop in the air at frequent intervals.

The original *Quickstep* design had a gaff cat rig, with a long gaff, a short boom, and the mast a foot or so forward of the place shown here — a cheap and effective rig all well inside the boat's guards. The Humber yawls weren't called so on account of rig; the reference was to yawl-boat; still, they mostly did have yawl rigs and I thought the new design would be prettier if it had one. The idea shown, of picking a rig out of a popular one-design class,

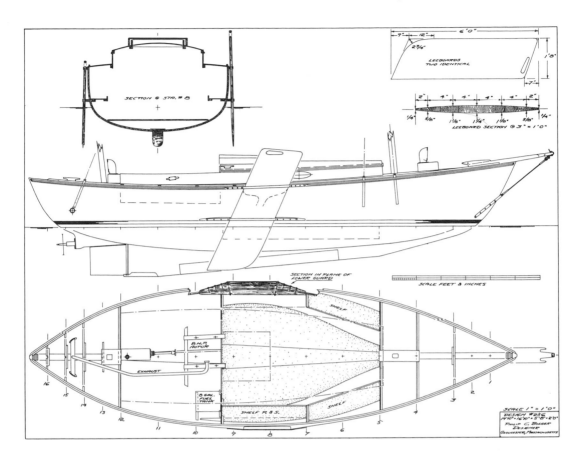

can save a lot of work or money, especially if you can get in touch with a red-hot racing fleet where the boats keep discarding their old rigs in the heat of competition. I once rigged a sharpie yawl using the mainmast, sail, boom, and all from an obsolescent Star and the jigger out of a condemned sailing dinghy. The skinny old Star mast broke the first season, as they're prone to do in that class, but the hardware and sails are still going, I believe, attached to a heavier new mast. Judging from the behavior of the spars in the bendy-mast Lightnings I see racing, the same process would be likely with this specification, hence the scarphed solid-spar drawing furnished. But this boat would be amenable to a wide variety of rigs; her balance is not all that sensitive, and one big advantage of leeboards is that if they turn out to need altering, in shape or placement, it can be done without major surgery.

Boats like this, if nicely finished and kept up, can be good investments, there being always a romanticist around, glad to take her off your hands. Besides, as pocket cruisers go, they're good sailers and good seaboats with much spirit and no vices.

KEY TO PLANS

1.   False keel sided 5″, tapered in to 3″ at about station #5, and to 1¼″ at rudder stock.

2.   Keel 1¼″ sprung plank, maximum width 7″.

3.   Stem and sternposts sided 3″, molded 2½″, laminated.

4.   Stem and stern caps sided 3″, sawn out in sections as convenient; ¼″ bolts and 3½″ screws to posts about as shown.

5.   Ballast casting lead, all on one section as shown; seven ½″ bronze bolts through keel staggered as much as possible.

6.   Shaft log from 5½″ x 5½″ x about 2′0″; ⅜″ and ¼″ bolts plus screws from outside planking; fit log carefully to sternpost and planking and glue in place.

7.   Skeg is part of stern cap, enlarged as necessary to take stern bearing.

8.   Sawn frames in ends of hull from ¾″ siding, molded about as shown; no piece more than 5½″ wide is needed.

9.   Bulkheads and partial bulkheads ⅜″ plywood with ¾″ fastening frames molded about as shown.

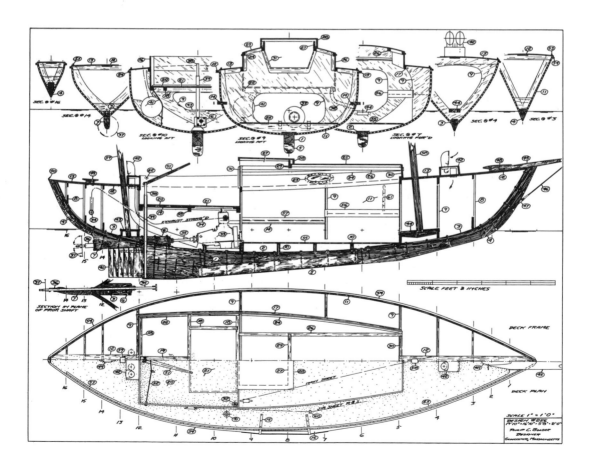

10. Floor timbers sided 1½″; ½″ bolts through false keel.

11. Planking ¾″ x 1″ strips, preferably soft pine or cedar but fir or mahogany may be used; set in seam compound or thick glue and edge nail with 2½″ galvanized wire nails spaced about 6″ and staggered 2″; 2″ bronze screws about every third strip to frames and bulkheads, and to stem and sternposts from every strip.

12. Centerline deck butt strap ½″ x 5″ plywood.

13. Deck ⅜″ plywood, fiberglass (or other plastic) sheathed.

14. Lower leeboard guards, inside and outside planking, sided about 1¼″, molded to fit planking; ¼″ x 1″ by about 3′9″ bronze or stainless steel strap secured with two ¼″ bolts and six 2½″ screws each side.

15. Upper leeboard guards 1″ with ends faired into sheer molding; straps ¼″ x 1″ x 3′3″ with 1½″ screws and 1/16″ x 1″ x 11″ straps over deck as shown.

16. Coaming and cockpit side walls ½″ plywood.

17. Carlings ¾″ x 1½″.

18. Sole beams 1½″ x 2½″; hatch carlings 1½″ square.

19. Butt strap ¾″ x 3½″.

20. Cockpit sole ½″ plywood.

21. Flush engine hatch, hinged across after edge, ½″ plywood; two dogs underneath at forward end to dog down watertight on a gasket.

22. Sole shelf ¾″ x 1½″.

23. Deadlights ¼″ clear plastic screwed to inside of coaming.

24. Trunk carling ¾″ x 1½″.

25. Trunk top ¼″ plywood, fiberglass sheathed.

26. Fore-and-aft beams from 1½″ square.

27. Hatch coaming ¾″ x 2½″.

28. Hinged hatch ½″ plywood; ¾″ x 1½″ frame.

29. Hatch beam from 1½″ square with crown cut from top side.

30. Forward end of trunk ¾″.

31. Companion slide ⅜″ plywood, dropping into slot between bulkhead and ¾″ x 1½″ cleats outside.

32. Cockpit scupper port and starboard about 1″ inside diameter with seacock on through-hull fitting.

33. Engine to be decided; shown is Palmer PW27, 8 h.p. @ 2800, direct drive, hand-starting; beds 1½″ x 3¾″ x 1′8″ hooked over floor timber each end.

34. Exhaust 1″ inside diameter tubing wrapped in asbestos or other insulation, led about as shown to 2″ inside diameter pipe out both sides of hull; put engine cooling water into pipe abaft high point under deck; no seacocks but flange carefully and provide stopper plugs.

35. Propeller shaft ¾″ diameter; bronze four-bolt stuffing box.

36. Bronze stern bearing (may have to be special) for Cutless rubber bearing.

37. Propeller 10″ diameter by 6″ pitch two-blade folding type.

38. Rudder stock 1″ diameter bronze, 3′10″ overall.

39. Rudder tube bronze about ⅛″ wall, to make stock an easy fit.

40. Rudder blade 1¼″; square trailing edge without taper.

41. Fuel tank to suit; shown 10″ diameter by 12″ long (four-plus gallons)

but may be much larger; flexible fill pipe to no-lose deck plate.

42. Ventilators: trap boxes on deck forward and aft as shown; 3″ throat swivelling cowls and deck pipes; deck pipes aft to be ducted low in the bilge near engine, to take out fumes, dangerous and otherwise.

43. Mizzen mast step ¾″ x 7½″ x 9¾″; 3″ screws at four corners.

44. Mainmast step from 3½″ x 5½″ x 1′7½″; 4″ lags at corners.

45. Bowsprit from 2″ x 7½″ x 3′5½″; 1′6½″ outboard; six ⅜″ bolts through deck; bed on seam compound.

46. Bobstay ¼″ stainless wire; lower end spliced round ½″ pin; upper end shackled to bowsprit end plate; measure and shackle in with bowsprit bent down by about 400 pounds weight on the end, to obviate need for turnbuckle.

47. Stem straps about ⅛″ x 1″ x 1′6″ stainless steel; five or six #14 gauge screws side to stem cap.

48. Jonesport cleat bolted through deck.

49. After cleat 8″ hardwood or bronze bolted through deck.

50. Strap for mizzen sheet block.

51. Tiller 1½″ x 2″ x 2′0″.

52. Dacron main sheet horse ½″ diameter.

53. Toe rails from ¾″ square.

54. Sheer moldings from ¾″ x 1″.

55. Cabin sole ½″ plywood; removable panel down centerline for bailing.

56. Shelf or locker port and starboard.

57. Shelf port and starboard on inside leeboard stringer; dining lap tables may hinge on the edges of these shelves or they can be closed in for fitted stowage.

58. Mainmast: see sail plan; though a Lightning rig is shown, any convenient one of roughly similar size will work, including masthead fore-triangle types.

59. Mizzen mast, unstayed; see sail plan.

60. Fairlead port and starboard for jib sheets.

61. Chain plates ⅛″ x 1″ x 1′3″ stainless steel; six ¼″ bolts through planking, each.

62. Leeboards from 1¼″ x 1′8″ x 6′0″ mahogany or Douglas fir; staves edge-nailed or drifted to center section; see enlarged section and diagram on arrangement drawing; provide pins to hold in full-up and full-down positions as well as the intermediate grounding-legs position shown, also a stop to prevent them from dropping out; no ballast is needed since the pins hold them against floating up.

Where material is not specified, any normal boatbuilding timber may be used; since much of the structure is designed to be glued or fiberglassed or both, oak, hard pine, and teak are generally to be avoided; except for the planking as noted, Douglas fir exemplifies the minimum hardness and strength expected.

25
YARROW

16'1" x 12'11" x 5'0" x 2'6"

Archibald Fenton had his boat shop at the head of Smith's Cove in Gloucester Harbor, and there he modeled and built a lot of extremely pretty
boats, among others Howard Blackburn's transatlantic singlehander *Great
Republic.* One of his last designs was a class of miniature Tancook whalers,
the last of which is Becky Garland's *Wind,* beautifully restored at about
fifty years of age. *Yarrow* is a close copy of *Wind* — not a take off; if I felt
like changing something, I changed it, but I didn't feel like it in many
places.

She's a docile boat with no treachery or wildness in her, predictable in
her handling and easy moving in a chop. Apart from her lovable looks,
her main virtue is that she can be sailed in a relaxed and absent-minded
fashion without being bitten, yet she still feels like a thoroughbred. Her
maximum speed is low, as a deep-bodied boat as short as this is bound to
be, especially with a sharp stern to rob her of effective sailing length and
power; the proper use for any such boat is day-sailing in a small area.

There's no good place to install an inboard engine, or to stow or hang
an outboard, in this tiny hull. With the oars and rowlocks indicated she
can easily be rowed a mile or two in an hour, and will seldom be caught so
far from home. Besides, she's an exceptionally good sailer in light airs and
I've given her a large and tall rig on the theory that people who would
choose such a boat would not usually care to sail in heavy weather.

Construction is conventional except for the glued-strip deck. I like the
looks of this deck construction and it's less apt to rot out than a plywood
deck. If plywood is used it might save some grief to flatten out the crown
abaft the cockpit, where the cocked-up stern otherwise makes a pronounced
compound curve. If I were to build one of these now, I think I would use
sawn instead of bent frames in the ends of the hull beyond the ceiling,
especially aft. To get away with not using a bobstay, that bowsprit must be
oak or something at least as tough; Nathanael Herreshoff used to show off

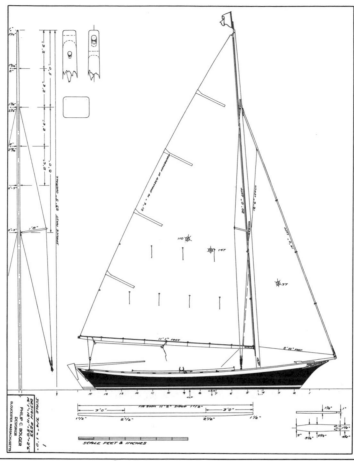

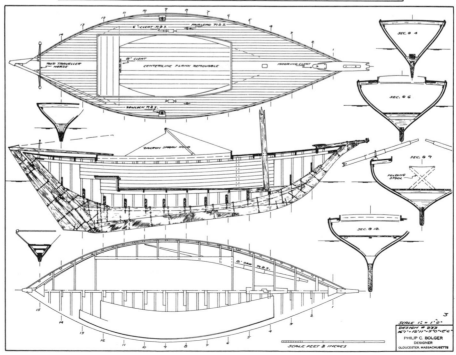

by using much longer bowsprits than this one without bobstays, in racing boats at that. Since even he wasn't quite infallible, sometimes one of them broke, but it's a fact that bobstays are the ugliest and most inconvenient fittings a boat can have.

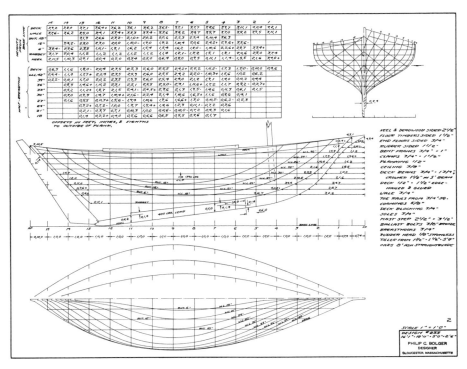

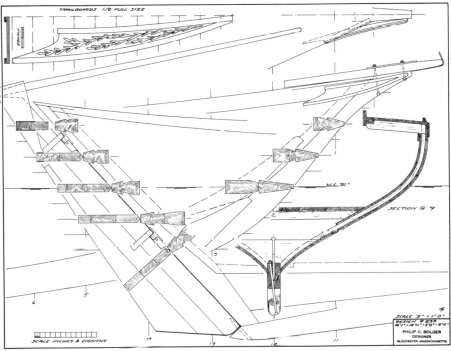

26

PRANCING PONY

22'0" x 18'8" x 9'5" x 3'11"

This design was made for a Maine boatbuilder who thought he might cash in on all the interest in Friendship sloops by putting out something with a more or less "period" style but much more roomy than anything looking like a real Friendship can be. I was thinking of a Bermuda sloop when I designed her, and if you'll look at the proper section of Chapelle's *American Small Sailing Craft* you'll know as much about those as I do. The first boat was delivered as a bare hull to some owner intending to finish her, and I've heard no more about it. I surmise that she is either still sitting unfinished in a shed, as often happens, or else is giving satisfaction.

Another one was built with a ferro-cement hull, rather nicely done to look at, at least. She was also delivered unfinished and that one I *know* is still in her finishing shed. In other words I haven't ever seen one sail, but as I take it nobody is likely to expect more than a modest sailing performance with a boat on these proportions I'm confident that no desperate disappointments will come of it. Any boat on these globular lines will meet with conditions fairly often in which she will bob madly up and down and not make much progress; also the speed at which she begins to bog down in her own waves is quite low, somewhere between five and six knots, a limit that applies under power as well as sail. On the other hand, her lines of flow are not so bad and she has a big rig, so it may be that she will get around in light and moderate weather better than you might think. As may be, she ought to be a hard boat to get into serious trouble with as long as you allow plenty of sea room, and considered as a weekend cottage she has some real attractions.

The high counter with small transom is nice-looking, and has the advantage of not being so sensitive to variations in draft as a big, deep transom. On four foot draft the displacement is upwards of 6,000 pounds (I've mislaid the exact figure) and I thought if about 1,400 pounds of lead were set in cement under the cabin sole the wooden boat might come out about that and have enough stability to get along on due to the great buoyancy. It certainly will not take much ballast to make her uncapsizable, always assuming it stays where you put it in a knockdown. Power to carry sail is another matter, but a boat of this kind can't be driven hard to much purpose in any case.

For the ferro-cement version, I figured the displacement drawing 4′5″ and got 9,200 pounds, which is more like the Bermuda sloops and which I judged would allow for as much ballast as she would be likely to need even with the weight of that construction. If she is actually ballasted as deep as that, she should become more dignified in her motion and very likely more weatherly, though still slower as to top speed.

No detailed specification was ever made as she's not the kind of boat for anybody to build who needs a detailed explanation of how to do it, and she is not at all critical on weight. The keel and all deadwood are on one siding, 3½″ oak, planking ¾″ mahogany, bent frames 1″ x ¼″ oak, decking ½″ plywood except around the cockpit and aft where it can be ⅝″ or ¾″ strip cedar or fir. The transom is a loftsman's nightmare in shape; if a transom like this is framed, it takes forever to build and always rots out;

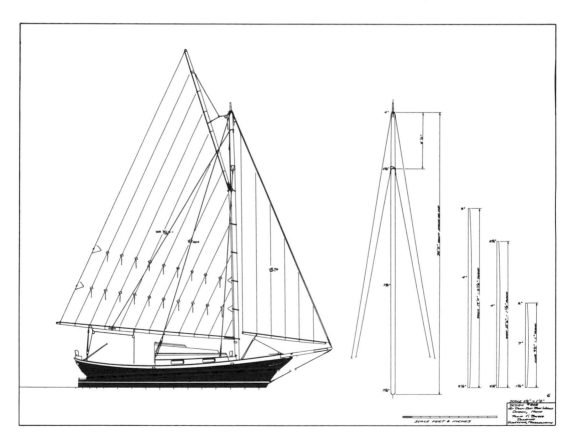

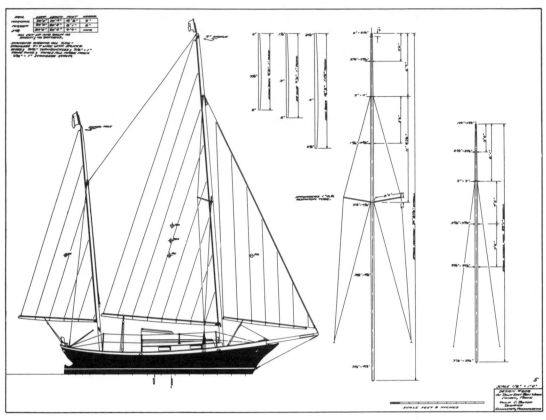

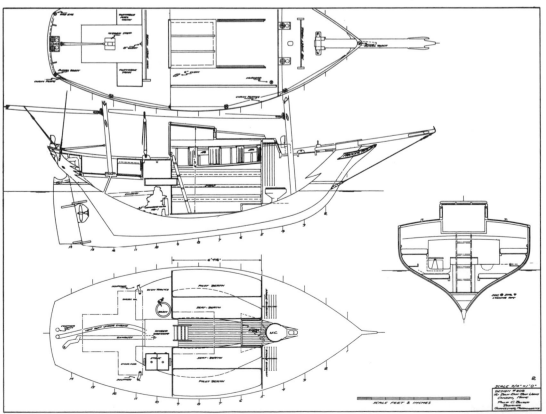

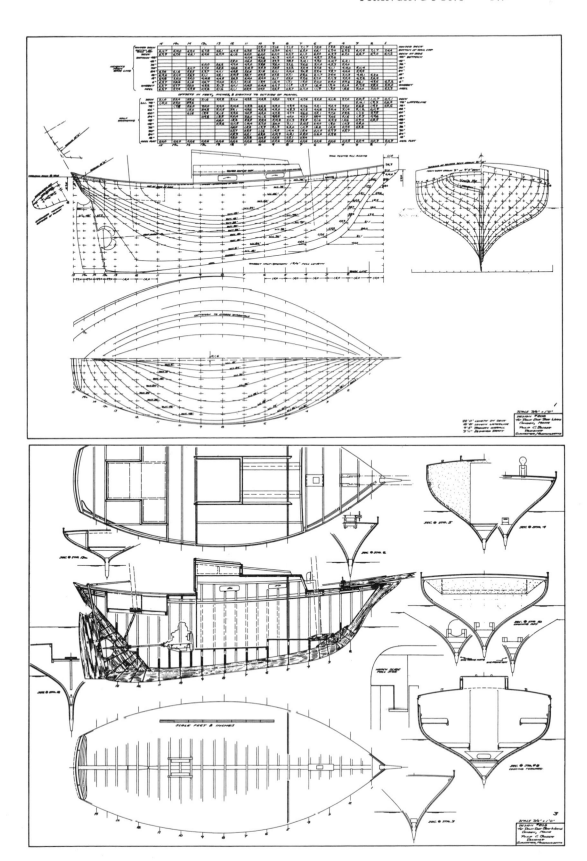

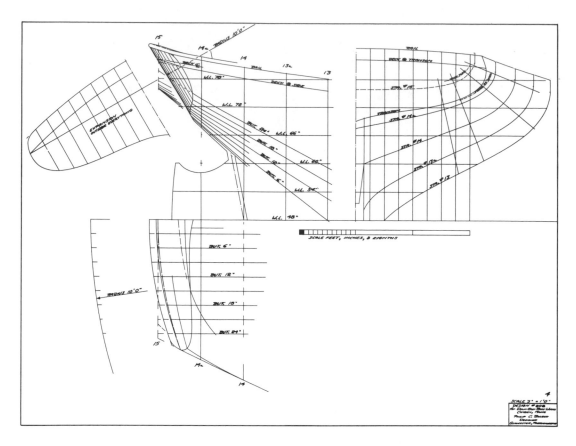

Prancing Pony *half planked*

this one is supposed to be built up out of edge-nailed sections sawn out to the given radius and carved to shape, without any frame. It's shown an inch and a half thick, cedar, but in building the boat it became clear that it ought to be substantially thicker, at least two inches, to get good fastening from the planking without a frame. There should also have been more deadwood inside the rabbet in way of the stuffing box than is shown.

The ferro-cement version created no problems at all and seemed to be a much more practical proposition, if it floats, as I suppose it probably will. I don't think this is the time to put out a cement specification, however, as the art is changing all the time and anybody who thinks of building an F-C boat should look around for the very latest publications on the subject. I'm inclined to bet that it will eventually be possible to build a boat out of this material that is not only useful but also reasonably good-looking.

The builder wanted solid masts, but the spar dimensions were meant to encourage the use of box-type hollow masts with about 3/4" forward and side wall and inch or inch-and-a-quarter after staves. No hardware details exist; sorry; Francis Herreshoff's designs are full of suitable stuff.

The gaff sloop rig was an afterthought but has considerable advantages. The jib is 24'0" luff, 21'0" leach, 9'2" foot; mainsail is 15'5" luff, 15'5" head, 18'5" foot, 31'6" leach, and 22'6" throat-to-clew. It's undoubtedly faster, more reliable, and cheaper than the ketch, and has a lot less windage. The ketch is easier to keep under control when maneuvering in a crowd and easier to induce to steer herself.

I consider this a sloppy design in the sense that I never really got around to finishing it after putting it together very hurriedly in the first place. Still it seems to me that if what you yearn for is a very comfortable cabin in a very short boat, you might go further and fare worse. I've certainly seen a lot of boats that were not nearly as pretty.

27

NAHANT

25′6″ x 8′8″ x 2′0″

This design began as a sketch intended to illustrate an article about dories I was writing for *Rudder* magazine. The article was mostly of the debunking kind as I was, and am, troubled at the mythology that's been built up around the word dory. The sketch was to show what kind of boat you get if you start modifying a dory to improve its sailing qualities, how the flat bottom becomes vestigial, the sides round out to a more and more pronounced bilge, and the long overhangs become shorter, until you end with a nice sailboat that is no longer anything like a dory and thereby prove that the dory was not a good place to have started. As it happened the sketch was not used with the article, but I became rather taken with it and took the trouble to more or less finish it off into a buildable design.

The result was what seems to me a rather nice shoal-draft cruiser, low inside but laid out to be quite respectable for a weekend or more for two or even three people. The combination of big skeg and big centerboard placed well forward provides good balance and easy steering, even self-steering with a little patience, I believe. Easy lines forward and plenty of lateral plane are indicative of weatherliness in rough water; she has beam and ballast enough to be quite stiff in spite of shallow draft and slack bilge; her propeller is placed where she can use her engine even though sharply heeled and pitching heavily, a talent which has been known to save lives in lee shore situations, among others. Although by recent standards she has a rather low freeboard, to the point of seeming quite graceful and a little old-fashioned, the raised deck brings all she has out where it contributes to reserve stability; in spite of being shallow as well as low, she has a good range of stability if the inside ballast is solidly secured, and there are few boats of her length more fit to go into open water.

The engine shown is just one that I happened to have a drawing of that was the right scale. Possibly a diesel's cost is not really good sense in a boat where long range is not of much consequence, though I must say that com-

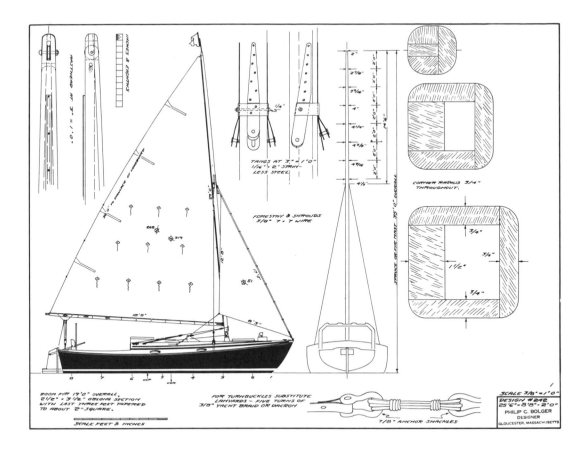

parative assurance against explosions is worth something to me even with the correspondingly increased fire hazard. As may be, she can take any engine in reason, the space not being tight and the weight placed quite low; also the propeller is placed where one even larger than shown would not completely wreck her ability under sail if it was two-bladed, and especially if the blades were feathering. In fact she might be regarded as a rather good type of small motor-sailer. She closely resembles a type of motor lobster boat that was common around Cape Ann for a few years each side of 1930, that I suppose were likewise derived from round-side modified dories.

The construction is something of a mess. I wanted it planked on sawn frames set up on the sprung flat bottom, dory-style, for the sake of illustration. Then, for some reason I've forgotten, I decided to show carvel planking instead of lapstrake, which meant that there had to be intermediate frames to keep the seams from working between the sawn frames. To save having to ribband her and drive a lot of nails into the sawn frames from the ribbands, I showed the intermediate frames very thin and screwed from inside. This is a construction most builders find repugnant, though

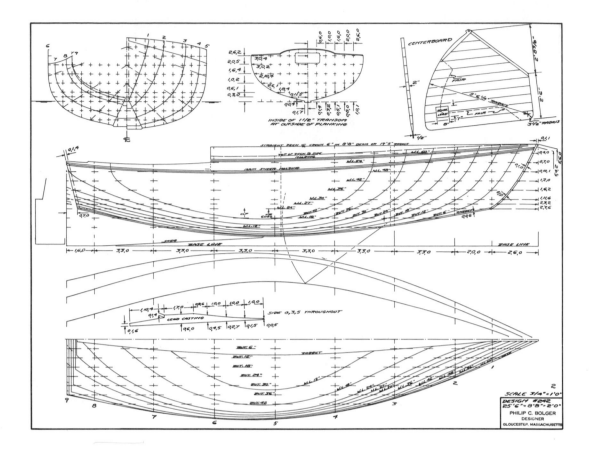

it does have the small advantage that you can ceil the bilgewater away from the berths with rather less loss of space than with more usual framing. I think if I was going to build one of these, I would either go to rather heavy strip planking or plywood lapstrake, say full inch for the one and at least a half-inch for the other, over the sawn frames without intermediates; or else have her all bent frames with temporary molds and ribbands in the usual way, with bent oak frames about an inch or inch-and-an-eighth by inch-and-a-quarter or a little more on around nine-inch spacing, or the 9¾ inches shown for the intermediates if the molds were on the given frame stations. I take it that nobody is likely to set out to build something as big as this without a fair amount of experience and well-formed ideas about how they like to go about it; please feel free to exercise prejudices.

As for the rig, the low and small jib is another legacy from the sailing dories. It's easy to sheet in, has minimum tendency to strain the hull, and its flow of air helps the part of the mainsail most likely to have stalled. Racing sailboats of the early and middle twenties were apt to have fore-triangles nearly if not quite this low, and it's illuminating to sail in one

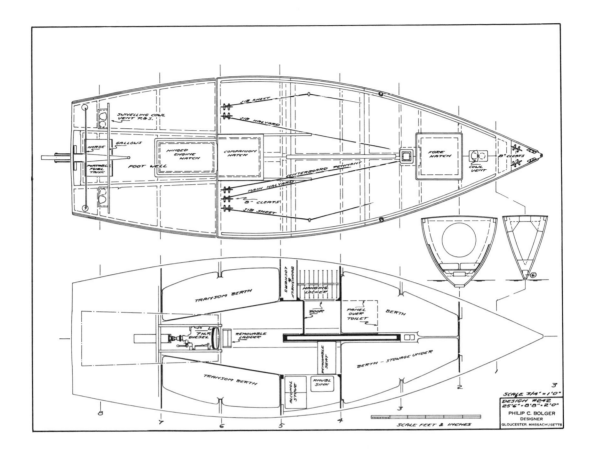

of them and see how she goes dead when you take the small jib off her.
It was the custom of limiting the allowable spinnaker by the size of the
fore-triangle that led to the steady increase in area there as fast as means
could be found to make the longer headstays stand. The low fore-triangle
made a moderate come-back in the sixties in bendy-mast dinghies; what
was sought in them was to throw a curve into the lower part of the mast
easing off to straight at the masthead, to pull the draft evenly out of the
triangular sail. This mast here should be too stiff to bend much and in any
case would have to be freed at the partners to produce a smooth curve; no
doubt the long unsupported masthead will whip some, but I haven't been
able to work up any enthusiasm for introducing compression bends into a
cruiser's mast. The proportions of this rig are due to the decision to use a
single shroud on each side, dispensing with spreaders for simplicity's sake,
at the available breadth, the shrouds can't go much higher than shown
without meeting the mast at so fine an angle that they strain the mast more
in compression than they support it against bending. The result is not very
graceful, but it's cheap and reliable.

KEY TO PLANS

1. Keel planks $1\frac{5}{8}''$ thick oak; two planks with splined seam on centerline; maximum total width $20\frac{1}{4}''$.

2. Skeg $3\frac{1}{2}''$ sided oak, tapered to $2\frac{1}{2}''$ from a little forward of frame #8; $\frac{1}{2}''$ galvanized bolts, drifts, and lags about as shown.

3. Ballast casting about 469 pounds lead with six $\frac{1}{2}''$ bronze bolts and two $\frac{1}{2}''$ x $8''$ lags. This outside lead is optional; skeg may be all wood with all ballast inside; see #42.

4. Lower sides of centerboard trunk sided $1\frac{1}{2}''$ Philippine.

5. Upper sides of trunk $\frac{3}{4}''$ Philippine edge-nailed.

6. Stem sided $3\frac{1}{2}''$ Philippine.

7. Block same siding as stem to take ends of clamps in place of a breasthook; bolt through stem.

8. Stem cap $1''$ x $2\frac{1}{2}''$ oak, steamed and screwed on over plank ends.

9. Headblocks of centerboard trunk $2\frac{1}{2}''$ square Philippine; note stopperblock to limit depth of board.

10. Sawn frames sided $1\frac{1}{2}''$, molded about $3\frac{1}{2}''$ and as shown, with $\frac{1}{2}''$ plywood bulkheads, partial bulkheads, and gussets.

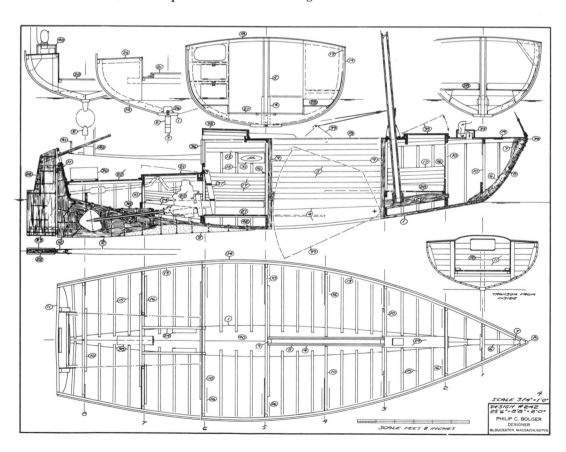

11. Transom 1½″ thick Philippine, edge-drifted, with 1½″ partial frame as shown; no frame needed across bottom as transom edge-grain will take the plank fastenings.

12. External sternpost sided 2½″ oak; transom bolts to the post and no knee is needed inside.

13. Clamps 1½″ x 2½″ fir or Philippine; at the break of the deck steam a bend into the ends of the clamps before installing them, to avoid a flat place each side of the break.

14. Planking 7/8″ thick, not less than thirteen strakes to a side to the main sheer; 1¾″ #12 Everdur screws to sawn frames, stem, and transom.

15. Intermediate frames ¾″ x 1½″ oak, steamed and bent inside completed planking and fastened from inside with 1¼″ #9 screws well countersunk; let heels into keel planks as shown, set in seam compound; stop clear of clamps at heads.

16. Stub frames next to sawn frames to take ends of ceiling, same as intermediate frames or smaller; need not be carried above or below ceiled area.

17. Ceiling ¼″ cedar; ¾″ #7 screws to intermediate frames; install between sawn frames in way of berths and lockers; see that air circulation behind ceiling between frames is not stopped by butt blocks; if a butt block must go under

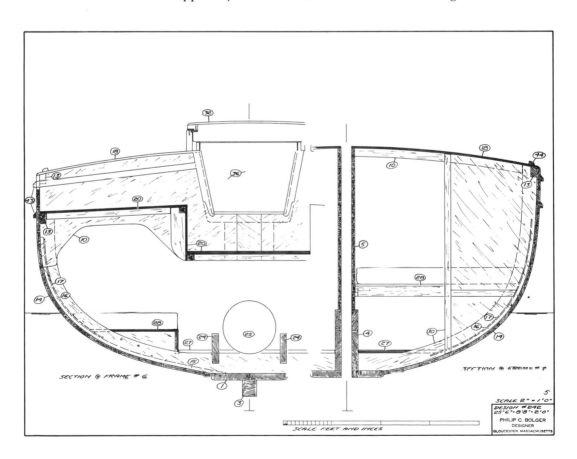

SECTION @ FRAME # 6

SECTION @ FRAME # 1

SCALE 2″ = 1′0″
DESIGN #242
25′6″-8′8″-2′0″

PHILIP C. BOLGER
DESIGNER
GLOUCESTER, MASSACHUSETTS

SCALE FEET AND INCHES

	9	8	7	6	5	4	3	2	1
Heights from base line									
RAISED DECK				4.10.0	4.10.2	4.11.5	5.1.6	5.4.0	5.5.0
MOLDING				4.8.0	4.8.2	4.9.4	4.11.4	5.2.0	5.3.5
MAIN SHEER	4.5.6	4.4.0	4.1.4	4.0.5	4.1.1	4.3.0	4.6.0	4.9.6	5.0.3
BUTTOCK 42"			2.6.0	1.8.1	1.5.5	2.2.5			
36"	4.5.6	3.2.0	2.0.4	1.4.1	1.1.5	1.7.6	3.6.0		
30"	3.2.0	2.8.0	1.9.2	1.1.4	0.10.7	1.3.6	2.5.7		
24"	2.9.6	2.4.4	1.7.0	0.11.5	0.9.1	1.1.0	1.11.4	4.10.0	
18"	2.7.0	2.2.2	1.5.1	0.10.2	0.7.7	0.11.0	1.7.2	3.3.1	
12"	2.5.0	2.0.4	1.3.3	0.9.0	0.7.0	0.9.4	1.4.1	2.5.3	4.6.0
6"	2.3.4	1.11.0						1.10.6	3.0.4
RABBET	2.2.6	1.10.1	1.1.7	0.8.3	0.6.6	0.9.0	1.2.0	1.8.4	2.1.0
Half breadths									
DECK	3.0.0	3.3.6	3.11.0	4.3.5	4.3.7	3.11.4	3.2.4	2.0.6	1.2.5
W.L. 60"							3.2.4	2.0.2	1.1.4
54"	3.0.0	3.3.6		4.3.5	4.3.7	3.11.4	3.2.0	1.11.2	1.0.0
48"	2.11.4	3.3.4	3.11.0	4.3.5	4.3.6	3.11.1	3.1.2	1.9.4	0.10.1
42"	2.9.2	3.2.1	3.10.6	4.3.4	4.3.4	3.10.7	3.0.0	1.7.2	0.8.1
36"	2.3.5	2.10.4	3.9.4	4.3.0	4.2.7	3.9.4	2.9.5	1.4.3	0.5.6
30"	1.3.3	2.2.7	3.6.0	4.1.3	4.1.5	3.7.6	2.6.1	1.0.4	0.3.3
27"	0.3.4	1.8.0	3.3.1	3.11.7	4.0.5	3.6.2	2.3.6	0.10.1	0.2.1
24"		0.10.0	2.11.0	3.9.6	3.11.2	3.4.2	2.0.5	0.7.2	
18"			1.8.7	3.3.1	3.6.3	2.9.7	1.4.0		
12"				2.1.1	2.8.5	1.9.4			
RABBET	(0.1.0)	0.2.7	0.6.5	0.9.2	0.10.1	0.9.0	0.6.4	0.3.2	0.1.2
	9	8	7	6	5	4	3	2	1

OFFSETS IN FEET, INCHES, & EIGHTHS
TO OUTSIDE OF PLANK.

DESIGN #242
25'6" x 8'8" x 2'0"

ceiling it should stop at least an inch clear of frames at each end.

18.   Deck ½" plywood in 4' x 8' sheets; 1½" #11 screws to clamps, beams, etc.

19.   Butt straps ½" x 6" plywood.

20.   Afterdeck and sides of foot well ½" plywood; well sole ¾".

21.   Hinged engine hatch ¾" plywood; note that hatch closes outside separate coaming.

22.   Rudder sided 2½"·Philippine; bronze pintles and gudgeons; Philippine tiller from 1½" x 5½" x 4'1".

23.   Stainless steel end plate screwed to bottom of rudder ¼" x 4" x 1'7".

24.   Engine beds to suit engine used; shown 1½" x 7" stringers and 2½" x 3½" beds for MD-1 diesel see #25.

25.   Gas or diesel engine 3 to 15 h.p.; shown is Westerbeke-Volvo MD-1 diesel with 1" bronze shaft, 12" diameter by 12" pitch two-blade solid propeller for about six knots. Bigger engines with larger diameter three-blade props would make a good motor-sailer but hurt her badly under sail alone; no engine and no hole in the skeg would improve speed and handling under sail substantially.

26.   Lead or bronze shaft tube about 1¼" inside diameter.

27.   Cabin sole ¾" plywood with outboard panels removable.

28.   Berth flats ½" plywood; 4" foam mattresses.

29.   Mast step 5½" x 7½" x 3'7" oak, with four ½" x 8" lags to frames.

30.   Outboard-type portable fuel tank about 12-gallon capacity; arrange motor connection to plug in cockpit.

31.   Deadlights ¼" clear plastic screwed to inside of ¾" blocks.

32.   Sliding hatch ½" plywood, same crown as deck; brass slide, for detail section see large-scale section #6.

33. Trap ventilator with 4" diameter throat.

34. Stem strap ¼" x 1½" x 12" stainless steel; three ⅜" x 3" lags to stem.

35. Hinged forward hatch ½" plywood, crowned with deck.

36. Companionway slide ½" plywood; fit with a louvered opening not shown.

37. Light ladder on lift-off brackets.

38. Shaft log from 5" x 5½" x 2'0" oak or Philippine.

39. Centerboard edge-drifted oak, 2" thick with ¾" diameter bronze pin; nipple in board to turn on pin; pennant ½" dacron, rigged with a four-part purchase on the tail consisting of a double block on the pennant and a swivel deck block with a becket just ahead of the belaying cleat; a simple winch may be substituted for the purchase.

40. Gallows double sawn to finish about an inch thick; bolted to trap boxes of after swivelling cowl vents. *Note:* if a gasoline engine is used these vents will have to be ducted under the engine and two more vents fitted; the additional vents might go close alongside the sliding hatch, and wherever they are it should not be far outboard where they could flood her in a knockdown.)

41. Traveller horse ½" round bar galvanized or bronze.

42. Ballast inside: from 1,000 to 2,000 pounds required according to amount outside and amount and position of other weights; preferably almost all of it should go in the #5-#6 bay, to accomplish which it must be lead and compactly arranged; I suggest that it be cast in slabs roughly 1" x 12" x 48", which can be laid athwartships, bending to the hull shape; nine of these slabs and the equivalent of four or five more in shorter lengths will fit under the sole, weighing about 800 pounds; the rest must go alongside the centerboard case or under the engine beds according to trim, with all of it bolted down to the keel planks or some other solid structure; a pump well should be left clear each side at the after end of the case. If all the ballast is inside or if it is iron and/or concrete, the cabin sole must be raised to give more space for ballast.

43. Philippine trim moldings from ¾" x 1½", beveled and drip-grooved as shown.

44. Toe rails ¾" x 1½" rounded off on outside and painted to blend into deck; they should not contrast as they would emphasize the powder-horn sheer produced by the plywood deck.

45. Chain plates ¼" x 1½" x 24" stainless steel, doubled over at upper end to take shroud shackle; not fewer than seven ¼" bolts through at least four strakes of planking, each plate; no internal reinforcement needed.

28

SEA HAWK DORY SKIFF

$$15'6'' \times 4'2''$$

Almost all the designs in this book were meant for slightly eccentric people who take a lot of their satisfaction in thinking about boats. This one is different, being intended for the type who needs a boat for fishing or transportation and isn't at all romantic about it. If he builds it himself he does it because it's cheaper that way, and if he buys it he doesn't mind at all if it was pulled out of a pile at a chain store, just so it will get him where he wants to go.

Harold Payson builds Gloucester Gull light dories and Thomaston Galley combination boats in his one-man shop in South Thomaston. These are the other kind, sold to scattered individuals here and there who like these "different" boats. But there also is a local market for him, a tiny segment of the international mass market for commonplace outboard utilities. Factory-built outboards are shipped thousands of miles to be sold in that locality; no doubt they're produced a lot more efficiently than a backyard shop can do it, but by the time factory overhead, shipping costs, dealer percentages, advertising expenses, and what-all are figured in, the selling price comes out about even. If the boat is a little better behaved than most of the big-production types and looks a little more shipshape, so much the better.

The flat-bottom shape with more or less flaring sides seems to me to make as good a light motorboat as any. Writers will have it that it's a hard-pounding shape, but I can't see that it's actually any worse than any of the more intricate bottoms; pounding is just a matter of how quickly the boat is stopped when she touches the water after a jump, and only an exaggerated deep-vee will spread this out enough to make much difference in this size range. Once you decide to have a shallow-bodied, stiff boat, the flat bottom is as good as any, and most of the peculiarities you see in the bottoms of boats in this class are partly to cater to prejudice and partly to stiffen up the limpness of thin plastic or metal. In this case, we wanted to use fairly

Sea Hawk *with a 7½ h.p. outboard (below)*
and 20 h.p. (above)

thick plywood to stand wear on rough shores and on trailers, and a plain, flat surface can be stiff enough and easier to keep clean and get around on.

The proportions were designed to make the slimmest boat that would be safe to stand up in, to make a cast or haul up a lobster pot. Keeping the boat narrow makes for light weight, for easy bends to speed up construction, for a sharp enough bow to punch through the crests of a small chop without being badly stopped, and for a small enough drag to be rowed some distance. The boat is no pleasure to row, but she's far from helpless under oars; running out of gas three or four miles offshore might be a considerable embarrassment, but she would get home all right a couple of hours and some blisters later if the wind didn't blow too strongly off the land.

I drew her with a good deal less flare of side than I've been in the habit of using in this type of boat, mainly because on a given breadth of bottom it's not so easy to get the gunwale under water, but partly because the more upright side allows easier lines forward. Being narrower on the gunwale also allows the use of short oars that are easy to stow out of the way. Otherwise she's just a slightly smoothed-up-square-tail semi-dory of a type I've done over and over.

She was tried with the twenty-horsepower-maximum motor, making about

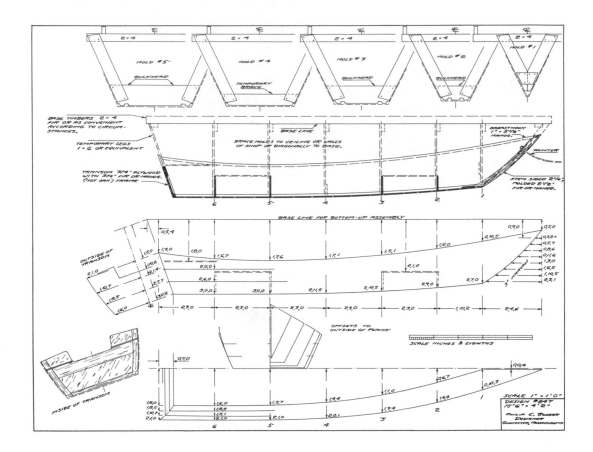

thirty miles per hour with two people and probably good for another five or more if a little study was put into propeller pitch. She didn't show any vices and carried the weight of the motor easily, but she certainly ought not to be given any bigger motor than that and I'd be much happier to stick to the 7½ h.p. motor with which she clocked fifteen knots. She seemed well able to take care of five people if they behave sensibly with that motor. In general she seemed an unusually decent little boat with no unpleasant surprises.

The spray rails on the sides were added to the plans after trials. I'd hoped to do without them and it's perfectly possible to do so, especially if you trim her bow-high, but the trials did make it obvious that she'd be appreciably drier at times if she had them. On the other hand, the builder doesn't like the quarter skids, which he thinks are too liable to get knocked off. What they're for is to make sure that in a sharp turn with power she doesn't start planing sidewise too fast, as can happen if the thrust of a powerful propeller banks her so much that the central shoe loses its hold of the water. I wish people wouldn't use that much power, or make such sharp turns,

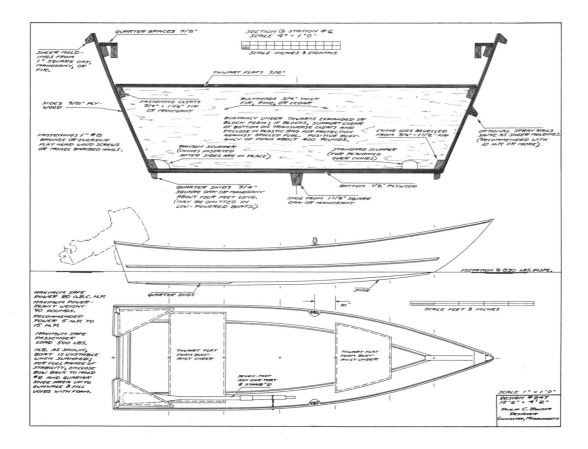

but since some insist on doing so I'd just as soon the skids were retained. They certainly ought to be fastened with care.

The prototype has Styrofoam buoyancy under its thwart flats. An experiment with some spilled outboard mix verified a dark suspicion that this liquid is not good for the foam, reducing a large block to a very small blob. I think the more expensive foam materials are worth the cost anyway, if only because they don't dribble their particles around so much, but it's just as well to protect any buoyancy material as well as you can from its surroundings, and to test its compatibility with them before you go too far.

In capacity this boat is closer to the general run of 12-footers than 15-footers; the stretch to a 15-foot length improves her running qualities and makes possible the very gentle curves and moderate bevels all through that make her an unusually painless proposition for an amateur builder as well as economical for a professional. She's also quite graceful to look at, whether her kind of owners care or not.

29

SEGUIN

15'6" x 7'1"

The original version of *Sequin* was designed in 1956. The seven-foot breadth was very extreme at that time but the results were much admired; a large number of boats were built to the design here and abroad by various builders. She resembles the Maine and Nova Scotia outboard lobsterboats now quite common; actually it is the other way around as she was one of the first designs for an outboard boat based on the larger inboard lobsterboats.

There were no complaints at all about the behavior of the original design, but there were a good many about the difficulty of planking the forward end. Wide boats with a strong chin to the forefoot are tricky to design and usually have a wicked bend in the first two or three planks above the garboard. In redesigning the boat I have fined her up in this region and recovered the buoyancy by a swell in the topsides higher and further aft; besides making her easier to plank up, this new shape has shown superior results in rough water wherever I've used it. The stern was not altered and only a few minor changes were made in the arrangement and construction. I'm of the opinion that the bent-frame and carvel plank method specified is both simplest to build and longest lasting where good bending stock is available; the design is of course suitable for strip or lapstrake construction, or for cold-molding. A permanent house in place of the spray hood would not do her much harm if it was kept reasonably light.

She can safely handle motors of fifty or sixty horsepower or even more, and will go as fast as anything of her size and weight with a given power. Twenty-five horsepower, or more if heavily loaded, would be about minimum to make what the old-timers used to call a "natural drift"; however, it's worth noting that a fast-type hull, if it has a good bow shape, suffers much less from being underpowered than a slow-speed hull like a rowing or sailing model does from overpowering. With, say, five horsepower, this boat would look unnatural and have a very dirty wake, but she will go practically as fast and behave about as well as most boats specially designed

Ted Sharp's original Seguin *with a 25 h.p. outboard*

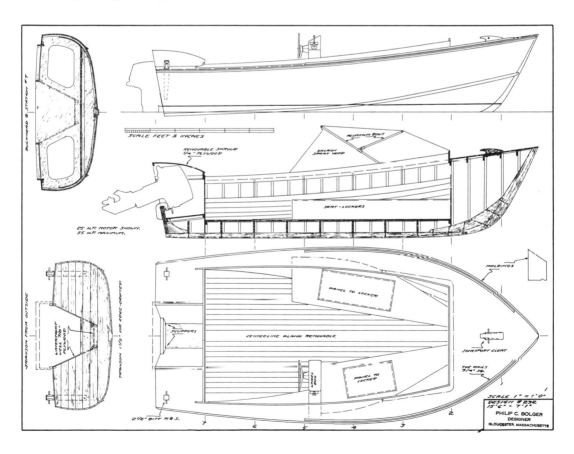

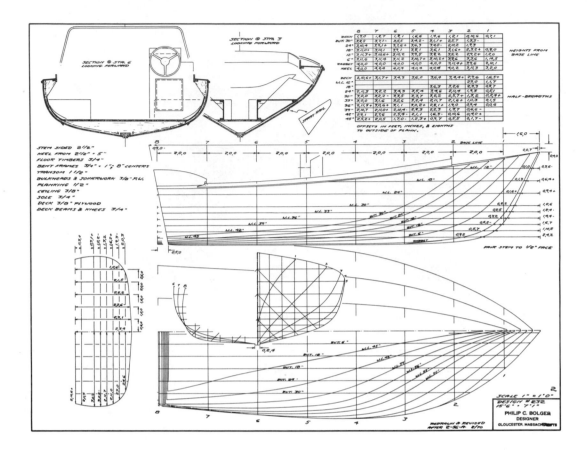

for that power; she will be much drier and otherwise more comfortable than the miniature tug and trawler models which are always uncomfortable and often dangerous.

It's futile to try to row a boat of this type; you break your heart and get nowhere. Carrying a small motor in reserve is perhaps sensible if the second motor is used enough to stay in running order. Unfortunately the usual cause of breakdown is a dry fuel tank.

30

HOPE

| 16'0" x 6'4" |

Hope is a working lobsterboat of normal type. She's thought by some good judges to be the best one of her class in these parts, but if that's true it's by means of small and conservative improvements. She was specially designed for the long-shaft eighteen-horsepower motor, very small power compared with what pleasure craft of her size are apt to have. The motor itself is light and she needs to carry little fuel, her weight as first put into commission being only about eight or nine hundred pounds all up. Soakage and accumulation of odds and ends will no doubt add a couple of hundred pounds in due course, and if she operates in winter she will need a shelter that will weigh another couple of hundred, perhaps, but even with such an increase she doesn't appear to need the spray rails indicated on the lines and construction drawings at her usual criusing speed of twelve or fourteen knots. At heavier loadings and higher speeds, she'd be drier with them, but the more powerful *Seguin* model would be a better choice in that case.

Ben Dolloff and I worked out her construction to try to speed up building and cut down maintenance. In a way she's a throwback, being the first strip-boat built without glue that I've seen in twenty-five years or more. The glue is so messy and so expensive, and it so often dries up before the strip is wholly secured, that it seemed worth a try to revert to the old methods and set the strips on an ordinary elastic seam compound. It's especially time this was tried because seam compounds are much better than they used to be, and because Anchorfast or other barbed nails can be mixed in among the edge fastenings or even used for all of them. I wanted to use a polysulfide (Thiokol) compound, but this was vetoed because of expense and because the stuff is almost as evil to handle as glue as far as making a mess is concerned, though there isn't the same risk of getting a dried-up joint.

So far, she's perfectly tight and seems as rigid as a glued boat. The cedar planking is a strong ¾" thick and should stand a lot of rough use. If she isn't quite as homogeneous in the shell as a well-glued boat, she has the

Owner and builder try Hope

advantage of more resilience in swelling and shrinking built into her; I once had the planking of a glued, mahogany-planked strip boat squeezed off the transom at the turn of the bilge when she swelled up, whereby she almost sank, and always find myself a little uneasy when trying to follow and deal with the stresses set up in boats of that construction. *Hope* ought not to have any such trouble and I'll be surprised if she doesn't prove a very long-lived boat.

Running the strips by the knife-edge stem and shaving a flat for the stem band off the end-grain is distressing to the designer because he can't dictate the precise profile of the stem and has to depend on the builder's eye. With Ben Dolloff doing the building, I wasn't worried, and with somebody I trusted less the work saved would justify some slight defects in the looks of a workboat.

The garboards were attached to the keel and stem bottom up; then she was turned right-side-up for stripping. If I'd been doing it, I would have done all the planking bottom up and saved some finicky business getting the molds in alignment after turning her, but the trade-off is against having to drive so many nails up from below. Incidentally, the molds used were made of heavy shipping-crate cardboard with a few wood cleats to take clamps, an idea Ben first used when he built the *Defender* dinghy.

The construction plan sheet shows the arrangement I tentatively suggested, with a high flush deck bailing out through the transom. I argued that this would make it easy to keep the usual sculch from accumulating in the boat, and leave the owner with an easy mind about rainwater; also she could be steered without the usual wheel and remote controls and leave an immense (for her size) clear space to carry the traps. Some railings would be needed and some kind of table the right height for a working bench. The men who had to do the work said that this scheme went to show that it'd been close to thirty years since I'd hauled a string of pots, or I'd remember how much difference even a few inches of height make in picking up and hauling, especially without a power hauler. The arrangement drawing, made after the fact, shows about what was actually done; it works well, of

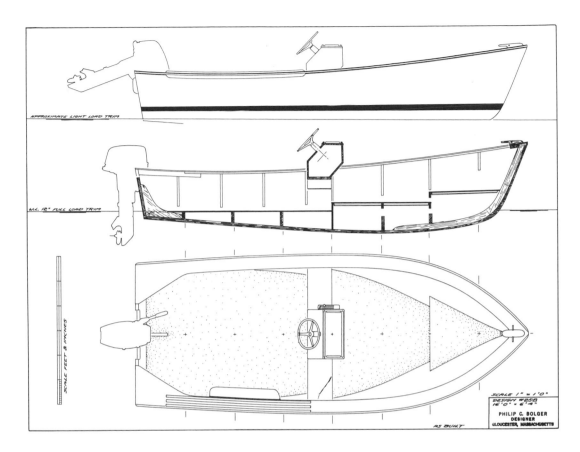

course, and the boat still seems roomy even with the thwart and console in the way, but I can't say I'm entirely convinced that I was wrong; I'd like to see the self-draining arrangement given a fair trial. And whether it worked for lobstering or not, it would make a spectacularly roomy utility.

Set up in Ben's cellar, the boat seemed enormous. A lot of people who came in to look at her thought she was too big for the motor. However, she shrank as they always do when moved outside and everything fell into nice proportion. The fact is, the size of motor you commonly see on boats this size around marinas is an outrage to common sense and makes you wonder about the future of humanity.

When the above was written we hadn't yet had a speed trial; I wrote what I and others estimated as her speed, 12 to 14 knots. In fact, the most usual estimate was 15, flat out, as she planed cleanly with no rooster tail. I planned to rewrite it or insert the correct speed later, but it seems to me now to be more instructive to let it stand, and add this note, that we ran the boat over a mile and got five minutes, fifty seconds one way and five-forty-five

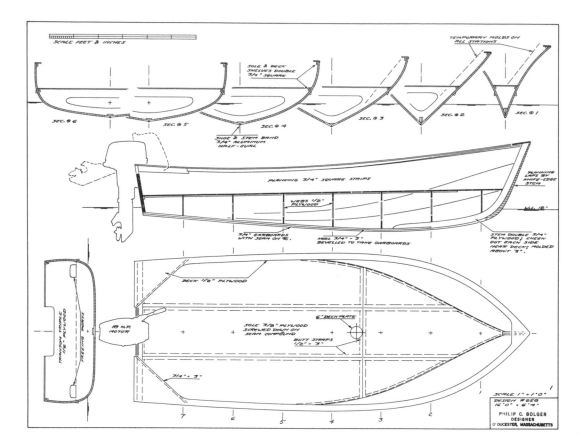

the other, with two men aboard with a small amount of gear and a reasonably clean bottom; in other words, somewhere between ten and a quarter and ten and a half knots, if anything nearer the former. You'd think at my time of life I wouldn't get caught this way any more, but I did, along with several other experienced people. Notice that the boat had been in use for some time before the trial and that nobody had noticed that it took longer than would seem reasonable to get around, nor had she seemed slow in comparison with other boats.

Apart from the general point that hardly anybody is going as fast as they think, and that statements elsewhere in this book concerning estimated speeds might be taken with some skepticism, it's of interest to observe that the real top speed of *Hope* is, in knots, about 2.65 or 2.7 times the square root of her waterline length in feet; this is the "speed-length ratio" which compares the wave-making characteristics of different sizes of boats. A boat 36 feet on the waterline would make the same kind of wave pattern at 16 knots; one 64 feet on the waterline at just under 22½ knots. The result is that very small boats look deceptively fast. I once saw a striking example: the *Coronet,* a schooner built for an ocean race in 1888, about 140 feet overall

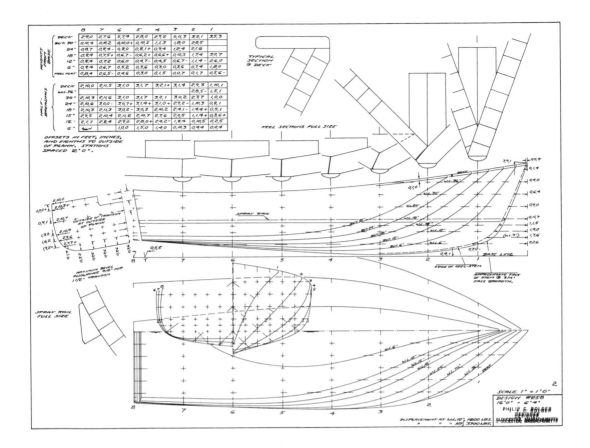

with no overhangs to speak of and very racy lines along and under the water, was coming up Gloucester Harbor under power, looking rather stodgy with her cut-down stumpy rig. There was a small feather of spray at her forefoot and an eddy following her, both almost imperceptible from a distance. Alongside her was a modern power cruiser of 30 feet or so roaring and throwing spray and to all appearances "planing," but barely keeping level with the schooner. Presumably both were making about 12 knots.

One more point: *Hope*'s speed in statute miles per hour is about 12. If you fall into the habit of using this figure but calling it knots, and then remember that it would sound much better in statute miles and translate to 13.82, rounded off as 14, and so on, you soon come up with a very comfortable figure.

31

CHIPPEWA

20'0" x 7'9"

I was prowling along the waterfront in Marblehead when I came in sight of a group of boating industry luminaries headed by C. Raymond Hunt, all looking intently at a small outboard motorboat which Hunt had apparently just brought in to a float. Spying at the boat, it seems to me I recognized it as a portent, though perhaps the recollection is colored now by knowing that the unpretentious little boat was to be the ancester of all the deep-vee types.

However that may be, I certainly did go home and think hard about the possibilities of giving powerboats a great deal of reserve buoyancy close above the water in combination with plenty of depth towards the centerline, which I thought, and still think, was the fundamental principal of Hunt's development. I had been trying to do the same job with a flaring side from the waterline up and had run into speed limitations. At the time I saw the Hunt prototype, I'd nearly decided that it would never be possible to build a really fast boat with a soft ride.

At the time, or soon after, I had an order to design a tender for an isolated camp on the Canadian side of Lake Superior; to this boat I applied the lesson about buoyancy, which fitted my earlier ideas so well that I was not tempted to copy Hunt's boat. I remember that I sketched the spray strips that were to become characteristic of deep-vee boats on the preliminary sketch, but then concluded not to have them on the boat unless and until it was proved that they were necessary; it seemed likely that the warped sections with concavity might do the job adequately.

The design I produced was that presented here, except that the stem and keel were dead straight and met almost in a sharp angle, as the photo shows. This was a bad mistake, which I built into another and larger boat before I realized that the straight keel was the cause of the wild steering the owners complained of, rather than some defect in the steering linkage as I'd first thought. Eventually I figured it out and have corrected it in retracing the plans.

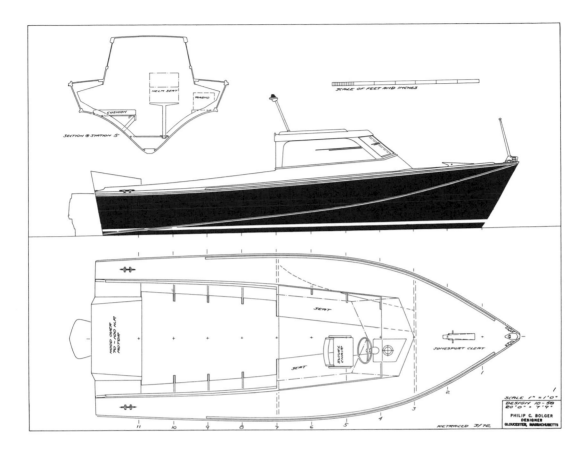

The boat made 32 statute miles per hour with a 75-horse outboard. She proved able to maintain 16 miles an hour on a run of 130 miles of open water in any ordinary weather, and she continued dry and buoyant when forced to slow down still more by really heavy weather. Dr. Rose, her owner, was high in her praise and would have been perfectly happy if it hadn't been for her exasperating tendency to yaw around, usually, of course, at the worst possible moments. He also thought that the narrow house was ugly and after a year or two had it widened. I have let it alone on the plans, partly to save myself trouble and partly because the reason for the original design still seems to me to be valid, namely that in coming alongside a wharf or another boat under rough conditions there's much less chance of trapping a crewman up against it or of damaging the house itself; it's also slightly lighter, though that would be a very minor consideration.

The boat was rather roughly built, workboat fashion. For a boat of her intended speed she's quite heavy in the skin. Strip construction has the advantage that you're putting the weight where it does the most good against the possibilities of hitting driftwood, which I take to be the biggest hazard of high-speed surface craft; not that the thickest skin is likely to do you much good if you run over a telephone pole at twenty knots, of course. I've shown a laminated stem, but the original design called for a double sawn stem without a knee, similar to others shown in the book. The double garboard specified was needed in the original boat because of the quick turn at the forefoot; as redesigned it may not be necessary, and if it can be got in without steaming, or if the builder doesn't mind steaming it, I'd prefer to have a single garboard as being less of a rot hazard.

Since I did this boat I've pursued the type through some fourteen years and I suppose forty or more designs, trying all kinds of variations: more and less S-shape in the sections, more and less keel rocker, sections with no hollow flare below the chine, hulls with all these types of section running out to perfectly flat sterns (these last being meant for low and medium speeds), and hulls with the chine rounded off on a big enough radius to make the boat appear almost a normal round-bilge type. After all this I'm not sure any of them were substantially better than this one all around, at least if you mean to go for very high speed.

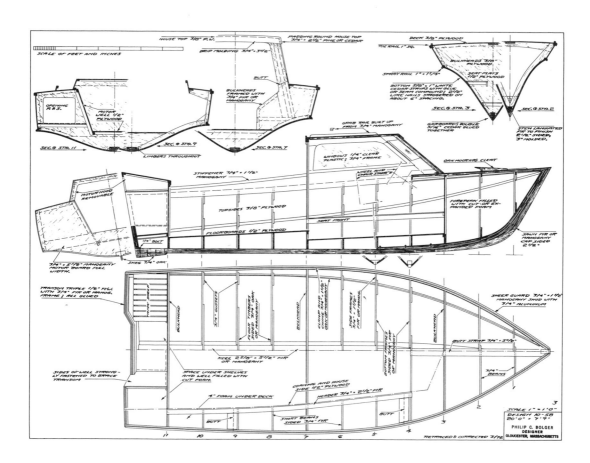

It hasn't really been demonstrated in a fair trial, but I think it's likely that the varying deadrise in all my designs of this type makes their resistance higher over a wide range of speeds. The warpage of this one is not extreme, but in some others where it was so there was some loss of speed over what I expected. With adjustable planing boards under the stern, the warpage is no longer necessary to stabilize the boat at high speeds, but I plan to go on using it in moderation because I think it makes for a softer ride at speed and for less of the quick, corky roll at rest that all boats with this kind of buoyancy tend to have. There's no question in my mind that the elimination of the fashionable multiple spray rails, skis, or whatever you want to call them, was a good move; given a properly faired and reasonably fine bow, they do no good except possibly at impractically high speeds, they make the ride in a chop noticeably bumpier, and, in my opinion, they make most boats wetter by tearing up the water far forward where it has time to bounce up again and blow inboard. A rail at the breakaway point, as here, usually is worth something, and now and then I've had to add a small rail running parallel with the waterline abaft the stem; these I think are a sign

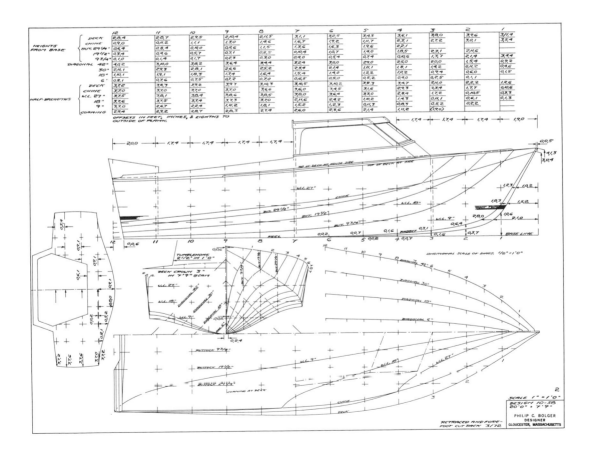

Chippewa *at full speed*

that the bow is not faired quite right, or that the stem is too thick or blunt in the face, or that the boat is badly trimmed.

Between being an old design, using a fairing method and type of offsets diagram that I've abandoned in the meantime, and having been a good deal pulled and hacked around in modifying the bow, it could be that these plans are no paragon of accuracy. I suggest that nobody plan to cut any corners in lofting one — good advice at all times, notwithstanding my efforts here and there to make the shortcuts less risky in some of the other and more recent designs.

32

HALLOWEEN

25'6" x 6'10"

This design was made for viewing the 1967 America's Cup races, and was meant to be the most economical boat that could comfortably maintain fifteen knots offshore in ordinary summer weather, and be reasonably safe if it should breeze on hard. In the end she was not built, but I'm still of the opinion that the design is one of the best I ever made.

The proportions were arrived at by taking the proven predecessor of the *Seguin* design and stretching it ten feet, mainly to enable her to go through a choppy sea faster and more comfortably, but also to carry more weight with the same power, to throw less spray when slowed down, and to be easier to plank up. Since breadth, depth, and scantlings were not increased, the weight of the long boat is only about two-thirds more than the short one; although she seems lightly constructed for her length, those same scantlings seem heavy in the fifteen footer, which is actually under greater stresses in rough water due to its coarser lines.

For some reason it's very hard to get the point across that there is an important distinction between a large boat and a long one. Thus some will complain that this design has very little room in her for a 25-footer, forgetting that she has a great deal for her cost and capabilities, and others will say she is too big to be a good trailer boat without noticing that she weighs no more than a great many of the twin-motor 18 and 19 footers often trailed. As to this last point, there's no doubt at all that extra length is helpful in launching and hauling up; on some ramps the long light bow of this design could be brought up on the first rollers without running the trailer wheel bearings under water. However that may be, if somebody is thinking of making more of a cruiser out of her, they ought not to plan on a higher or heavier cabin house than is appropriate for a boat under seven feet breadth

Apart from the lengthening, I gave the boat a much harder bilge in the after part of the hull than the *Seguin* original. There's no question in my

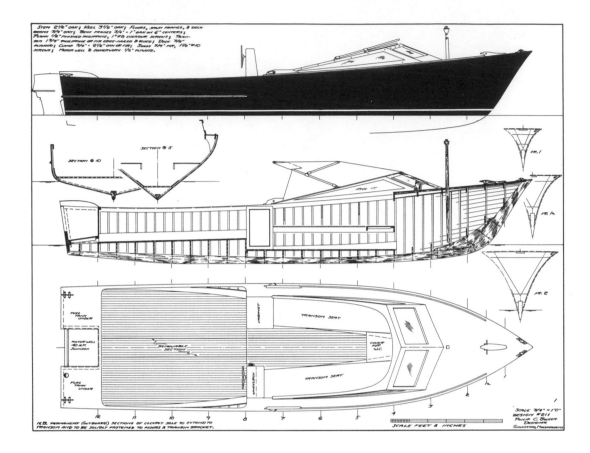

mind that this tends to leave a cleaner wake and to track better in a following sea than the slacker bilge, but it does mean that only the very best bending stock will take the shape; alternatively the frames could be bent double, or as a last resort replaced by sawn frames with gussets. Other constructions are perfectly feasible as with *Seguin*, and in this case the design was partly meant as a prototype for a fiberglass production hull; this was not proceeded with as the builder concluded that a bulkier boat would sell better.

It would not be hard to adapt this design for a light inboard with stern drive, or for that matter a straight-drive inboard if it was kept well aft and the tank put in the stern. Personally I think the simplicity of installation and convenience of maintenance much favor the outboard motor in boats of this type.

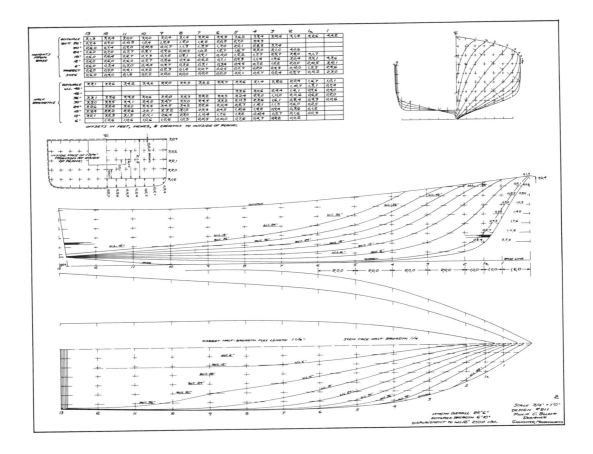

33

DESTRIER

28'0" x 11'0" x 2'2"

This model is one that I used with variations in a large number of designs, certainly more than fifty; I abandoned it quite abruptly after the *Chippewa* proved out, because the new type was better able to stand heavy loads, exaggerated power, and the high bridges and towers people were beginning to insist on having. This older type needed to be relatively light displacement for the overall dimensions or it would quickly bog down and become wet and hard to drive, and it lacked the initial stability to carry weight high up. Still a lot of people became very fond of boats of this type: the Egg Harbor 31-footers, for instance, change hands seldom and at high prices, not entirely because of their exceptionally good construction. All the type were very easy in a head sea at moderate speeds; they might pitch deep, but they never brought up with a bump. They also had an easy roll which made them more comfortable for trolling in a swell than the more buoyant later type. They drive easily with relatively low power.

What I'm driving at in all this is that, though this design is obsolete in a sense, it still has the making of a nice boat to use if you don't overstep its limitations. I'd be happy to see more of them built if I could count on their not being half-sunk with twin engines, or a diesel, or made top-heavy with added superstructure. This particular design was elaborately worked out to be exceptionally light, with glued lapstrake planking and minimum frame; it was meant for production, but at a low rate, three or four boats a year. The project was aborted by financial problems but there's no doubt in my mind that it had good potential.

Looking over these old plans, I see very little needing alteration. The engine specified is not available now, but any automobile light V-eight of around the power noted will do; the bridge can be built higher if necessary to give height for down-draft carburetion. Current standards for gasoline power call for a couple of intake vents beyond what is shown, and the overboard-flushing toilet is no longer smart even where it may still be legal; a

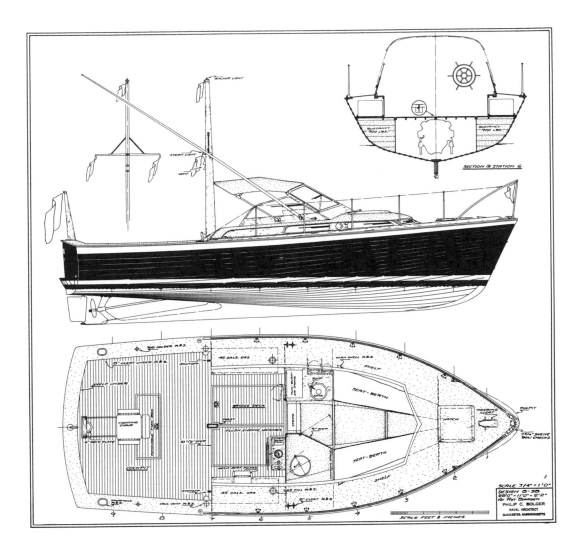

portable toilet seems more suitable for her type than any built-in type with or without an integral holding tank. This cabin would be a pleasant enough place for a couple of people to spend a week-end in, but I don't think it would help to start trying to elaborate it. Making it shorter and smaller, or eliminating it altogether, would be a better way to go.

If kept to the designed weight, this boat should have a top speed of about thirty M.P.H. with 225 h.p., and an easy, smooth, and quiet cruising speed of twenty knots. She will still run cleanly, handle well, and be exceptionally dry, at speeds right down to idle. Few boats will maintain more speed against choppy water with less hardship on her people, and few will maneuver as neatly in tight and crowded places. She's more suitable for less power than for more; she would make a natural drift with quite small engines, down to 100 h.p. or even less if the power plant is correspondingly light and she isn't crowded with people or other weight; reduction gearing should be adapted to a propeller not much smaller than the one specified. Incidentally, I should think that she might do well with an outdrive or a couple of big outboard motors, presumably with a flat transom in place of the much-rounded one designed, and most of the skeg faired away; she might or might not need trimboards or planing wedges at her stern to keep the forefoot from lifting too much.

KEY TO PLAN

1.   Skeg and outer stem sided $2\frac{7}{8}$″ fir; may be laminated or scarphed up from solid timber; stem band $\frac{1}{2}$″ half-round chromed brass; a removable metal or wood grounding shoe, not shown, should be placed all along bottom of skeg.

2.   Inner stem laminated fir to finish sided $3\frac{1}{2}$″, molded 3″.

3.   Keel apron from $1\frac{1}{4}$″ x $7\frac{1}{2}$″ fir; may be double $\frac{5}{8}$″; transom knee sided $3\frac{1}{2}$″ shaped to take rudder port flange.

4.   Bulkheads and web frames $\frac{3}{8}$″ fir plywood backed with $\frac{7}{8}$″ fir; bulkhead at station 7 and web frames at stations 8 and 9, with temporary extensions to sheer line, will serve as planking molds; other mold stations must have temporary molds.

5.   Transom double $\frac{1}{4}$″ fir plywood (mahogany if to be finished bright) with $\frac{7}{8}$″ fir fastening frame; 3″ x 4″ scupper with hinged flap port and starboard.

6.   Transom radius beams sided $\frac{7}{8}$″ fir; lower takes after ends of cockpit sole beams; upper with facing to form shelf take lower edge of three $\frac{7}{8}$″ knees supporting deck across stern.

7.   Clamp $1\frac{1}{4}$″ x $1\frac{3}{4}$″ fir set inside planking.

8.   Outer clamp/sheer molding $\frac{7}{8}$″ x $1\frac{1}{2}$″ beveled on top to take deck and on under side to $\frac{3}{8}$″ face below bottom of deck; $\frac{3}{4}$″ half-oval chromed brass molding.

9.   Planking $\frac{1}{2}$″ marine grade waterproof fir plywood, twenty-one strakes to a side more or less; about $1\frac{1}{4}$″ laps, bolted and glued without holidays; throughout the boat all joints and seams should be liberally glued, including berth and shelf flats which are structural.

10.   Deck double $\frac{1}{4}$″ fir plywood, fiberglass sheathed; angle of deck and trunk side might be filleted and glass carried up side.

11.   Deck blocking for cleats, stanchions, etc. $\frac{7}{8}$″ fir.

12.   Knees under deck in way of cockpit $\frac{7}{8}$″ fir.

13.   Deck beams sided $\frac{7}{8}$″, molded $2\frac{1}{2}$″ fir.

14.   Web knees $\frac{3}{8}$″ plywood with $\frac{7}{8}$″ fir frame.

15.   Angled beams to carry trunk front same as other deck beams.

16.   Facing of cockpit $\frac{3}{4}$″ x $3\frac{1}{2}$″ fir or mahogany (Philippine).

17.   Toe rails from $1\frac{1}{4}$″ mahogany, height as shown, beveled on outer side to $\frac{3}{4}$″ top face.

18.   Deck header $\frac{7}{8}$″ x $2\frac{1}{2}$″ fir.

19. Trunk rising 1¼″ x 4½″ mahogany, beveled to tumblehome of side.

20. Cockpit and bridge sole ¾″ rift-grain clear fir in about 2″ strips laid athwartships, finished natural; secure with screws to be removable without too much wrecking to get at steerer, exhausts, etc. flush hatches as shown and as judged needed edged with 1″ chromed angles; bridge hatches fitted with drain channels piped overside.

21. Strong beam 1¼″ x 1½″ fir.

22. Sole beams ⅞″ x 1½″ fir, resting on web frames.

23. Block and socket for small fighting chair.

24. Boarding step and rest for dinghy ¾″ mahogany, supported by about nine knees or metal brackets; this step shouldn't be built up of openwork or any way pierced as there would be danger of the dinghy scooping the exhaust inboard.

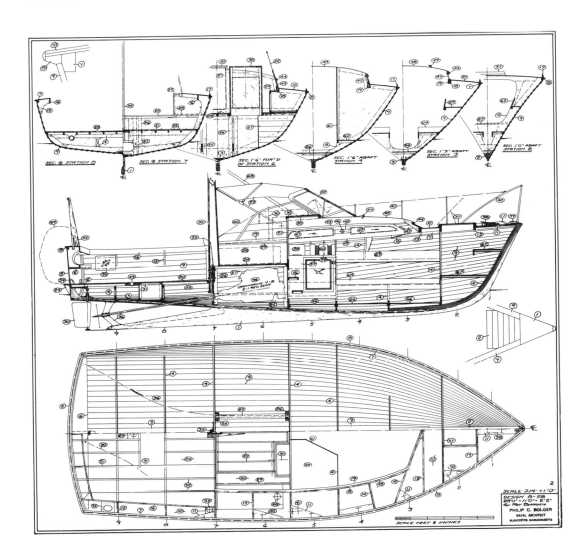

25. Engine bearers built-up tee section; $1\frac{1}{4}''$ cap glued and bolted to $1\frac{1}{4}''$ vertical; cap $3\frac{1}{2}''$ wide, vertical $5\frac{1}{2}''$ deep; vertical extends $2\frac{3}{4}''$ beyond cap at each end.

26. Ends of vertical engine bearers nipped between two vertical $2\frac{3}{4}''$ square posts at each end; posts glued to bulkheads and bolted through bulkhead and backing; engine bearers held by two $\frac{1}{2}''$ bronze bolts through each pair of posts.

27. Styrofoam or similar buoyancy material packed outboard in bilges (also under decks, berths, shelves, etc., wherever convenient to increase minimum 1,800 pounds positive buoyancy furnished by that shown in engine compartment), held and faced with celotex or other sound-absorbent sheet, with which bulkheads and planking in engine compartment (and elsewhere as and if convenient) are also to be lined.

28. Monel or fiberglass fuel tanks $12''$ deep, $18''$ wide, $4'0''$ fore and aft inside dimensions (about 45 gallons each); fuel lines emerging from top of tanks with

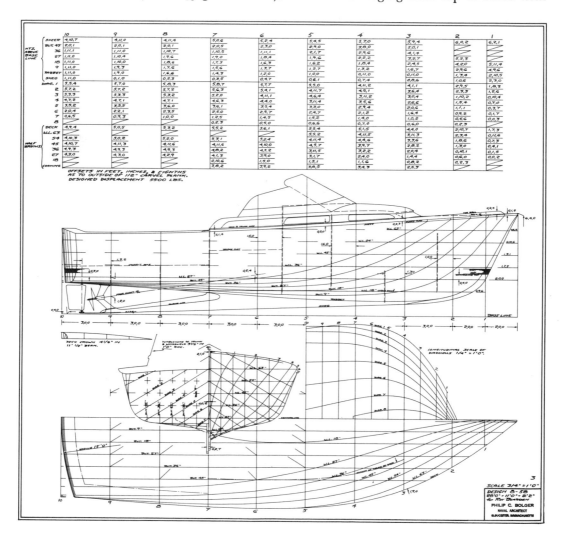

shutoffs in cockpit as shown as well as at engine; ¾" inside diameter vent tubes out topsides as high as possible; fill pipes with "no-lose" deck plates as far forward as possible.

29. Sealed compartments for tanks; walled and floored air-tight from hull, bridge, and deck with glued sheet plywood; vented and drained overboard through scuppers out topsides at each end as shown on outboard profile drawing.

30. Columbian #605 or similar cast bronze rudder; ¼" x 2" bronze skeg; oval base bronze rudder port; Marmac dynaflex steerer to 24" overall diameter six-spoke wood wheel.

31. Removable fish box ½" plywood, fiberglass-lined; flush hatch same construction as cockpit sole.

32. Cleats in cockpit 8" bronze "Sea-grip" or other bronze or wood to taste, bolted to ⅞" fir pad fitted to inside of planking; 4" x 6" oblong hawsehole in deck above well rounded off all ways.

33. Cowl vents about 3" throat diameter set in exhaust position not less than 48" abaft gas fill pipes, and ducted to bilge under engine; one or the other to have manually operated electric exhaust blower set high under deck in cockpit.

34. Vent opening port and starboard above level of boarding platform cowled to bilge.

35. Mast hollow; ¾" mahogany side panels tapered from 8" to 3" at truck; headblocks ⅞" x 1½", with additional blocking at foot to take two ½" bronze bolts through bulkhead; foot held by 3/16" x 1" bronze strap; forward of bulkhead foot of mast to be open to engine compartment to form a somewhat unnecessary vent with louvers below 4'0" tip-to-tip yardarm braced from above only.

36. Graymarine V-8, 225 h.p.; 2:1 reduction gear; rubber mounts; 1⅜" monel shaft; Morse flexible coupling; flexible-neck stuffing box on bronze shaft log; special cast bronze strut with Cutless rubber bearing; 18" diameter by 20" pitch three-blade propeller of wide-blade high-speed design; engine saltwater cooled with Aqua-Clear Feeder or freshwater cooled with Sen-Dure system or other internal heat exchanger; exhausts taken as far outboard as possible port and starboard, with rubber silencer on each; Graymarine All-in-One instrument panel; Marmac Model G reverse and throttle controls mounted on flat-topped 3'11" high mahogany wheelbox; note that wheelbox is open underneath and hatches fitted around it; access to interior to be via a large panel in bulkhead opening into toilet room.

37. Forward hatch with continuous hinge on after edge and adjuster to brace open in any position; fit with screen.

38. Mahogany mooring cleat with brass pin, bolted through deck blocking.

39. Skene-type bow chocks.

40. Special chromed brass pulpit; forged steel stanchions like Merriman #670, 24" high to center of eyes; plastic-covered wire-rope lifeline not less than ¼" overall diameter, set up with turnbuckles at after end.

41. Midship 8" bronze cleats.

42. Mahogany flagstaff with brass tongue set in flush socket.

43. Trunk sides ¾" mahogany.

44. Shim on trunk side ¾" fir shaped to fit lower edge of molded top.

45. Mahogany ¾" backing and window frames of trunk side and front.

46. Vent 2" diameter; clam shell opening aft on trunk side.

47. Fixed windows of ¼" plate glass or clear plastic in sides and front of trunk.

48. Molded fiberglass-reinforced plastic trunk top.

49   Continuous grab rails of mahogany serve to stiffen trunk top; not less than four through-bolts each.

50. Double-hinged companion hatch hooks back against windshield; fit with screen.

51. Double-hinged door folds away port side; use plenty of vent louvers in one section or both; screened.

52. Metal or wood windshield preferably not too flimsy to hang on to.

53. White canvas or nylon navy top; bows with W-C or similar fittings to fold down on forward side of windshield.

54. Navigation lights W-C "Wing-Tip" type forward, stern, side, and anchor lights; cabin lights to be chosen by builder with owner's approval.

55. Folding seat for helmsman blocked up about 6" above top of tank boxes.

56. Companion steps lift off brackets.

57. Dresser with locker and three shelves about as shown.

58. Two-burner alcohol stove.

59. Stainless steel sink or basin; hand pump piped to freshwater tank under cockpit forward of station 8.

60. Dish racks as the spirit moves.

61. Toilet enclosure ½" fir plywood lined with some sound-insulating material; mirror inside door; hooks for hanging on forward side.

62. Toilet sole ½" plywood raised to about level of waterline 27"; fit shelves under deck as the need appears.

63. Seaclo "Skipper" toilet or galvanized bucket.

64. Berth flats ½" plywood; 4" airfoam mattresses.

65. Shelves ½" plywood faced with ¾" mahogany.

66. Cabin sole ½" plywood in three removable sections between webs; might surface with cork tile.

67. Slatted shelves ¾" fir for rough stowage.

68. Fiberglass or bamboo outriggers.

69. Dinghy 9'0" x 3'6".

70. Spherical compass in binnacle on wheelbox.

71. Danforth Hi-Tensile 18-pound anchor in chocks.